THE
New Testament
HANDBOOK

New Testament Handbook
© 2024 Holman Reference
Brentwood, Tennessee
All Rights Reserved.

Typesetting and design by Faceout Studio, Sisters, Oregon.

Style	ISBN
Sage Cloth-over-Board	978-1-0877-9135-7
Stone Cloth-over-Board	978-1-4300-9453-1

DEWEY: 220.02
SUBHD: BIBLE—HANDBOOKS, MANUALS, ETC.

Printed in China
1 2 3 4 5 6 7 8 9 10 — 30 29 28 27 26 25 24
RRD

Contents

Letter from the Publisher

The Bible has a lot to say about beauty and how beauty might serve as a means leading to the praise and worship of God. In fact, just looking at the Old Testament narratives involving the construction of the tabernacle and the temple, we come to realize that there is a lot of specificity and detail surrounding their craftsmanship. The detail of these designs and the level of craftsmanship involved were not merely meant to create a place that instructs God's people—those designs and the beautiful creations that resulted were also meant to point the congregation to God's glory. When the Lord told Moses, "Make holy garments for your brother Aaron," he said to make these "for glory and beauty" (Exod 28:2). In other words, these craftsmen and artisans of the Old Testament were instructed to complete their tasks for the combined effect of both glory and beauty.

Unfortunately, too often the notion of beauty is overlooked in Christian culture. However, it is good to be reminded that the medium should always be commensurate with the message. Since Christians have the most beautiful message, the one found in the pages of Scripture, it is incumbent upon us to create beautiful mediums that relay that message in hopes that they also point others to the glory of God.

The *New Testament Handbook* before you seeks to do just that in a creative and informative way. Intended to be used as a stand-alone reference work and/or companion to individual Bible reading and study, the *New Testament Handbook* focuses on presenting important biblical themes, theological concepts, and individual book summaries in a visually compelling way. Its presentation of synthesized biblical material through intentional design and infographics helps deepen one's understanding of the historical, literary, and theological context of each book of the New Testament. Features include the following:

- One-Sentence Summaries
- Book Introductions, Outlines, and Genre Indicators
- Word Studies
- Maps
- Timelines
- Charts and tables connecting Christ and key themes across Scripture
- Infographics about key figures and events
- Key Verses and Key Quotes

The *New Testament Handbook* is intended to enhance your reading and understanding of the beauty found within the pages of the New Testament and ultimately point you to "God's glory in the face of Jesus Christ" (2 Cor 4:6).

Andy McLean
Publisher

Connecting and Completing the Story:

THE ORIGIN AND CANON OF THE NEW TESTAMENT

Imagine walking into a play at the beginning of the third act. Not an ideal experience, right? You might be able to pick up on certain elements of the plot and piece together who the most important characters are, but no matter how well you paid attention to the third act—and unless you had already seen the play—you could never compensate fully for what you missed during the first and second acts. Sure, there are some prominent themes you might be able to delineate, and you might piece together something about the conflict based on seeing the resolution emerge. Nevertheless, you still would not have the acquired familiarity with the whole story that the playwright intended. Much the same could be said about how we should approach the New Testament in view of the Old Testament.

To understand what the New Testament (NT) is, then, we need to understand what the Old Testament (OT) is. That may seem obvious enough. After all, how can we have a *new* without an *old* (see Heb 8:7–13)? And despite how some might treat the the OT and NT as two separate stories, when understood properly, they come to us telling one unified story: creation, fall, promise, and fulfillment.

The OT presents us with a personal, self-sufficient God making a good world (e.g., creation) that was then corrupted through humanity's rebellion (e.g., fall). Rather than leaving this world in its self-afflicted misery or immediately destroying it, God in his grace enacted a plan to redeem and restore his creation and to do so primarily through the family of Abraham, who later became known as the Israelites (e.g., promise). This earlier part of the story constitutes what we call the OT. Following the high-stakes drama that befell this family-become-nation, Israel, over the centuries, God would bring his Son, Jesus the Messiah, into the world to complete his plans of redemption and restoration (e.g., fulfillment). This latter part of the story constitutes what we call the NT.

So, when we think of the NT's relationship to the OT, we should not think of it like a spin-off TV series or even a movie sequel. Instead, we should see the content of the NT as the final act of a play, the climax and resolution of the Bible's larger storyline. In other words, the NT sees itself as the completion of the OT story, a story that is from beginning to end centered on Jesus. As the apostle said regarding Christ and the promises of God: "For every one of God's promises is 'Yes' in him" (2 Cor 1:20).

OT	NT
CREATION →	NEW CREATION (not yet)
FALL →	REDEMPTION (accomplished and applied)
PROMISES →	FULFILLMENT (already)

MESSIAH (Jesus)

TOWARD A DEFINITION: GOD'S (INSPIRED) WORD ABOUT GOD'S (INCARNATE) WORD

In the introduction to the *Old Testament Handbook*, we considered the following definition for the OT: *God's timely and inspired Word*. The latter adjective, "inspired," refers to the process by which the Holy Spirit supernaturally and concurrently worked in the human authors of Scripture to produce the message God desired down to the words themselves (2 Tim 3:16–17; 2 Pet 1:19–21). Inspired authors wrote inspired texts, giving these writings a unique identity and a unique authority as God's Word.

The former adjective, "timely," possesses multiple senses when used to describe Scripture. God's Word is timely, first, because it functions as a record of God's speech and revelatory acts in history: an eternal, infinite God communicating in time and space (2 Kgs 17:13; Jer 7:25; Dan 9:6; Hos 12:10; Luke 1:1–4; Heb 1:1–2; cp. Acts 26:26–27). Second, God's Word is timely because God's authoritative revelation always comes at the "right" time regarding his redemptive purposes (Deut 30:11–16; cp. Rom 5:6; Gal 4:4). Third, God's Word is timely because it is forever relevant as God's authoritative revelation for all time to his people and to humanity in general (Gen 1:26–30; 2:15–17; Pss 1–2; 1 Cor 10:6–11).

Because God's revelation of himself in Christ took place "when the time came to completion" (Gal 4:4), we can see how it is especially timely in the second sense. As the completion of the OT story, the NT affords us the capacity to build on the previous definition when taking the full corpus of Scripture into consideration. Yes, from the OT we may observe that Scripture is God's inspired and timely Word. However, in view of the NT and its claims about Jesus, we can expand our definition to the following: *God's timely and inspired Word in the form of a collection of writings that bear witness to Jesus the Messiah, God's eternal and incarnate Word*. The NT, in other words, is the timely climax and decisive conclusion of God's special revelation that indicates to us that all of Scripture, OT included, is centered around the person and work of Jesus the Messiah (Luke 24:25–27,44–47; John 5:39–40,46; 2 Tim 3:15). Jesus, the eternal Word who was with God and who was God, became human both to reveal and to redeem (John 1:1,14). Accordingly, the inscripturated Word centers on the incarnate Word.

How then does this definition help us think about what the NT is, where it came from, and which books truly belong to this portion of the Bible? We will consider this in three stages. First, we will look at how the NT sees itself in continuity with the OT. Rather than as an abrupt interruption to the OT story, the NT presents Jesus's coming as the Messiah and his institution of the new covenant as the conclusion to this story. In other words, the story of the OT was left unfinished, and the NT came about to finish the story. The writings of the NT accordingly operate as the announcement that God's ancient promises have found their zenith in Jesus and the new-covenant community that he established.

Second, with the establishment of the new covenant, it follows naturally that a body of literature would emerge to govern this new-covenant community, defined by their allegiance to Jesus and heeding his commands (Matt 28:19–20). In short, a covenant requires a canon of sorts, or a set of governing documents, so to speak. This is precisely the reason a particular set of books became what is known as the NT. But how do we know which books should be regarded as authoritative covenant literature?

When we get to the third stage of our discussion, we will consider how the NT canon commends itself as God's self-authenticating Word and how the Holy Spirit works within the life of God's people to bring about widespread recognition of the NT writings' divine origin and status. Before considering the scope of the NT's content (i.e., canon), however, we should first consider the substance of the NT's content (i.e., claims).

"SEE, THE NEW HAS COME": THE GRAND FINALE OF THE OLD TESTAMENT STORY

As discussed above, the NT came into existence because the OT leaves its readers with an unfinished story. The OT is a play looking for its final act. It is a collection of books that instill the reader with expectation and longing. From the onset of sin, God promised an offspring that would defeat the serpent's toxic grip on humanity. He would soon promise to extend blessing to all peoples and nations through this offspring and later would promise to manifest his sovereign and just rule through a righteous king who would come from this same lineage.

Perhaps the following list of questions regarding God's purposes and promises can help us see the apparent continuity and intentional incompleteness of the OT story:

- Who will *rule* over the earth (Gen 1:26–28)?
- Who will strike the *serpent's* head (Gen 3:15)?
- Who will *reenter* the garden through fiery judgment for us (Gen 3:23–24)?
- Who will be *Abraham's offspring* who will bless the nations (Gen 12:1–3; 17:3–8)?
- Who will be the ruler from the line of *Judah* (Gen 49:8–10)?
- Who will be the *prophet* like Moses (Deut 18:18)?
- Who will be the king from *David's line* who will bring about an everlasting age of justice and peace (2 Sam 7; Ps 89)?
- Who will be the *Suffering Servant* who will bear our iniquities (Isa 52–53)?
- Who will establish a *new covenant* with God's people (Jer 31:31–34; Ezek 36:24–27)?

Given the portrait of the Messiah and his eschatological work that the OT paints for its readers, it should not seem like a stretch to anyone to see why the NT authors perceive Jesus as the subject behind the portrait. He is the true image of God who conquered Satan, death, and sin (Col 1:15; 2:14–15; Heb 2:5–9,14–15; 1 John 3:8), Abraham's true offspring who came to bless all nations (Gal 3:16), David's greater son who has come to rule his kingdom with righteousness and justice (Matt 1:1–17; 22:41–46; Luke 1:32–33), and the mediator of a new and better covenant (Luke 22:20; Heb 8:6–13; 9:15–22).

Furthermore, as the old covenant established through Moses came with a body of covenantal revelation to constitute the people's relationship with God, likewise, covenantal revelation came along with Jesus's institution of the new covenant. Stated less tersely, the events of the first exodus with Moses were recorded and presented in covenantal terms: "Moses took the blood, splattered it on the people, and said, 'This is the blood of the covenant that the LORD has made with you concerning all these words'" (Exod 24:8). Correspondingly, the events of the final exodus with Jesus, which came about through his atoning death on the cross, were also recorded and presented in covenantal terms: "In the same way he also took the cup after supper and said, 'This cup is the new covenant in my blood, which is poured out for you'" (Luke 22:20; see also 9:31; John 1:17). The OT came into existence as a record of God's covenant acts in the history of the people of Israel along with being revealed instruction to them as a covenant community. The NT similarly came into existence as a record of Jesus's life, death, resurrection, and ascension along with being revealed instruction to the church as the new-covenant community. In short, the OT announced to Israel that Yahweh is King and what that meant for the people; the NT announced to the world that Jesus is King and what this means for the church.

In a dramatic (yet not completely unanticipated) turn of events, the coming Messiah was revealed to be the Creator himself, Israel's God known as Yahweh (e.g., Pss 45:5; 110:1; Isa 9:6; Dan 7:7–14). The Messiah, then, was sent from God yet also God (e.g., John 1:1). Accordingly, as Yahweh commissioned the Israelites to be a "light to the nations"

(Isa 42:6–7; 49:6), Jesus charged his followers to proclaim his dominion and authority over all nations as Lord (Matt 28:18–20). As participants in the third act of the story, our roles primarily involve living as ambassadors for our once-crucified, now risen and ascended King (Acts 1:8; 2 Cor 5:20–21).

APOSTLES AND PROPHETS: THE CANONICAL SELF-AWARENESS OF THE NEW TESTAMENT AUTHORS

Given God's past covenant dealings with his people, we should expect a covenant body of literature akin to the NT so that God's new-covenant people would have something that would function like a covenant document as their standard for faith, life, and worship. Though not comprised of a law code like the Mosaic covenant found in the Pentateuch, the NT nonetheless serves as a diverse, authoritative collection of writings that record formational events pertaining to the new covenant as well as providing instruction rooted in the church's new-covenant identity.

We see such an awareness of this reality regarding the writings of the apostles and their associates within the NT. As the apostle Paul articulated, the apostles saw themselves as "ministers of a new covenant" in contrast to the old (2 Cor 3:6). The Gospels, written from the perspective of these new-covenant ministers, are presented as something of the "authorized version" of the Jesus story, even based on their introductions and conclusions (see Matt 1:1–17; 28:16–20; Mark 1:1; 15:39; Luke 1:1–4). The apostle John's writing indicates an apostolic self-awareness as well, such as in 1 John 1:1–3:

What was from the beginning, what we have heard, what we have seen with our eyes, what we have observed and have touched with our hands, concerning the word of life—that life was revealed, and we have seen it and we testify and declare to you the eternal life that was with the Father and was revealed to us—what we have seen and heard

we also declare to you, so that you may also have fellowship with us; and indeed our fellowship is with the Father and with his Son, Jesus Christ. (See also John 21:24.)

Additionally, Paul placed his writing to be on par with that of a prophet: "If anyone thinks he is a prophet or spiritual, he should recognize that what I write to you is the Lord's command. If anyone ignores this, he will be ignored" (1 Cor 14:37–38; see also 7:12). Indeed, according to Paul, the teaching of the apostles was to be received not merely as human words but also as the word of God: "When you received the word of God that you heard from us, you welcomed it not as a human message, but as it truly is, the word of God, which also works effectively in you who believe" (1 Thess 2:13).

Moreover, when the NT authors acknowledged other writings from the NT, they regarded them as Scripture. Peter spoke this way of Paul's writing for instance:

Also, regard the patience of our Lord as salvation, just as our dear brother Paul has written to you according to the wisdom given to him. He speaks about these things in all his letters. There are some things hard to understand in them. The untaught and unstable will twist them to their own destruction, as they also do with the rest of the Scriptures. (2 Pet 3:15–16)

Observe these last six words: "with the rest of the Scriptures." This indicates that Peter thought of Paul's writings as Scripture because he referred to parts of the Bible other than Paul's letters as "the rest" of Scripture. There were Paul's letters, which some twisted and mishandled, and there were "the rest of the Scriptures" that these same persons also mishandled.

Similarly, we see this dynamic of equating NT writing with the OT Scriptures in Paul's quoting Deuteronomy 25:4 alongside Jesus's statement from Luke's Gospel: "For the Scripture says: Do not muzzle an ox while it is treading out the grain, and, 'The worker is worthy of his wages'" (1 Tim 5:18). While we should not be surprised that Paul would refer to a verse in Deuteronomy as Scripture, we should take note that he would put a statement from Jesus found in Luke 10:7 as being Scripture on the same level as the Pentateuch.

As shown above, long before definitive canon lists were discussed at any council or mentioned in any patristic letters, the NT writings already carried a functional canonical authority throughout the Christian community, at least where they were available, during the first several generations of Jesus followers. Nevertheless, the NT provides us with the grounds for confidence that the church came to recognize the correct books as Scripture while rejecting others. In short, the NT provides a theology of canon.

CONCEIVING OF THE CANON: WHEN AND HOW DOES A BOOK GAIN CANONICAL STATUS?

When does someone become a parent? At the moment of conception? Once a pregnancy test or ultrasound confirms there is life in the mother's womb? In the delivery room? Or perhaps there are some who feel that no one earns their parenting card until they've had to deal with toddlers and/ or teenagers. While someone might not feel the weight of parenting until sometime after bringing their newborn home, there are varying stages of "parenthood status" (if we may coin a new term).

Even when a couple is not aware that conception has taken place, in a strict, technical sense, they are parents because they have brought new life into the world that previously did not exist. However, they do not have a way of knowing until the mother shows symptoms of pregnancy or a pregnancy test shows positive. In a documented sense though, parents do not legally name the child or receive a birth certificate until after the birth takes place. Moreover, on an experiential level, life as new parents might not feel like it has begun until they bring the firstborn into the house for the first time. So, then, how does all this parenting paradigm talk relate to the NT canon? What hath Jerusalem to do with obstetrics?

Originating from a Greek term meaning "rod" (as in a straight stick used as a standard for measurement), the term *canon* refers to an approved list of sacred or authoritative writings. When applied to the Bible, the concept of canon relates to books that are given by God and uniquely inspired in their composition and status. The canonical status of the NT books can be conceived of (pun definitely intended) in an analogous way to the above examples of parenthood status. Just as when a child is conceived in the womb and the parents have no way of knowing immediately that they are biological parents, the writing of an inspired text would not be known to the church at large at its moment of composition but would be known only to God and, at least on some level and in certain cases, to the human author. Nonetheless, the inspired writing *is* canonical in a sense because of its inspired origin and status. Either the Holy Spirit inspired a text or he did not, and this is the case before any church or group of churches recognized its inspired status.

Further, before a book in the NT could be recognized widely as an inspired text, copies of the text had to first be distributed. Even before copies of all or most of the NT books were made available to churches across the Mediterranean world of the first three centuries, the churches that had access to some of them nonetheless regarded them as possessing inspired, apostolic authority regardless of whether churches in other regions had seen them. In this sense, a book carried canonical status in a functional way. The churches were not waiting around until formal councils were held and official lists were drafted to treat the books they had received as inspired, authoritative, and consequentially canonical. These books already held a canonical status in a functional and practical sense even if portions of the NT were not available everywhere for a time.

Finally, there is a more formal sense that the canon came into fruition on an institutional level once universal access to all 27 books became a reality. Among the writings of the church fathers of the first four centuries, for instance, we find an awareness of most of and sometimes all the 27 books with which we're familiar today. During the late first century, Clement of Rome likely had access to all 27 writings, and during the second and third centuries, Irenaeus of Lyon and Tertullian of Carthage each listed 22 of the books based on what we can observe. Eusebius of Caesarea, an early church historian, named all 27 books, and by the fourth century, Athanasius of Alexandria, the biblical scholar Jerome, and Augustine of Hippo each affirmed the same 27 books. The church fathers thus reflect both the reality of a functional canon existing among the churches as well as a formal canon taking shape through their naming and listing the authoritative books.

Eusebius's *Ecclesiastical History*: Four Categories of Christian Writings[1]

1) Recognized Books (Universally Received)
   - First century (connected to the apostles)
   - Four Gospels, Acts, Paul's Epistles (where Hebrews was included), 1 John, 1 Peter, Revelation

2) Disputed Books (Some Disagreement but Eventually Accepted by Most)
   - James, Jude, 2 Peter, 2–3 John

3) Rejected Books (Generally Orthodox but Not Seen as Inspired Canon)
   - *Acts of Paul,* the *Shepherd of Hermas, Apocalypse of Peter, Epistle of Barnabas, The Didache,* the *Gospel of the Hebrews*

4) Heretical Books (Widely Considered as Unorthodox, Forgery, and Impious)
   - Gnostic Gospels (second century): the *Gospel of Thomas,* the *Gospel of Peter,* the *Gospel of Mary,* the *Gospel of Philip, Gospel of Truth,* etc.
   - *Infancy Gospel of Thomas, Apocalypse of Peter, Acts of Andrew, Acts of John,* etc.

We should be sure to note, also, that no singular council of the first several centuries ever sought to determine the canon for all churches everywhere once and for all. No council would have seen itself as conferring inspired status or apostolic authority on any set of books; instead, the councils saw themselves as facilitating a discussion about which books had been regarded as Scripture among various churches. Despite what *The Da Vinci Code* might tell us, the Council of Nicaea (AD 325) did not determine which books became part of the NT, and for this matter, neither did the Councils of Hippo (AD 393) or Carthage (AD 397). While the canon was not a topic of discussion at Nicaea, the latter two councils merely affirmed the same 27 books that most churches in their geographic regions had already accepted as authoritative because of their apostolic origins and content by sometime in the fourth century.

We can now move from the *when* to the *how* related to the NT canon. We know something about the development of the process, so now we should consider *why* we should trust the process. In short, the same text inspired by the Holy Spirit is also illuminated by him in the hearts and minds of God's people so that they would be moved to heed it once exposed to these apostolic texts. The same Holy Spirit who worked in the authors also worked in the audience. Furthermore, Scripture, being the Word of God, cannot defer to any source outside of itself to derive its authority. Otherwise, God's Word would depend on something other than God himself and it would not be an ultimate authority. So, no criteria or council can determine Scripture's inspired status; these conventions can only recognize its inspired status.

Another way of putting things, the canon must be self-authenticating; otherwise, it must look to another "canon" (or standard) of sorts to support its claims of supernatural authority. Then we would need to know what makes this standard an authority and so forth, leaving us in a never-ending pursuit of verification for each external standard we might refer to. The canon instead must commend itself. Thankfully, the canon not only makes claims for itself, as we saw above regarding the NT authors' apostolic and canonical awareness, but for our sake, the canon also provides the basis for how we can rest assured that the collective church affirmed the right canon. Consider Jesus's words: "My sheep hear my voice, I know them, and they follow me" (John 10:27).

Put more descriptively, God works supernaturally within the hearts and minds of his people so that his Word will resonate with them (see 1 Cor 2:10–14; 1 Thess 2:13). Jesus likened this process to sheep recognizing their shepherd's unique voice. While there is no precise formula or advance metric for assessing whether a text is inspired, the strong consensus over the 27 books that emerged during the early centuries should give us great confidence that Jesus's sheep did indeed hear his voice uniquely in the 27 books that make up the NT.

The church thus was adequately faithful in this process not because of her own infallibility but because of the Spirit's illuminating and affirming work among her members. God's Word alone is infallible among texts, but the Spirit, who also is infallible, can work effectively even within a fallible and flawed church. The sovereign God who inspired his Word can ensure that it will not return empty; it will accomplish what he pleases (Isa 55:10–11). Part of God's purpose in inspiring and sending his Word is so that his people will know where to find it (Deut 30:11–14; Rom 10:6–8,17).

CONCLUSION

If God has ordained a role for us in his redemptive drama, we should trust him to provide the script and everything else we need to perform our respective tasks (Eph 2:10; 4:11–13; 2 Pet 1:3). And that's what the NT offers us: the message and mission that is the third and final act. The Bible presents to us one cohesive story centered around the person and work of Jesus the Messiah, the OT pointing forward to him and the NT announcing his arrival as King. Accordingly, the content of the *New Testament Handbook* is designed to give readers the same quality of content offered in the *Old Testament Handbook* with its literary analysis, word studies, timelines, tables, and infographics. These items have been designed and curated to deepen readers' understanding of and appreciation for the Bible as God's timely and inspired Word that bears witness to Jesus, God's eternal and incarnate Word.

Matthew

Genre | **GOSPEL, HISTORICAL NARRATIVE**

Jesus is the Messiah—the true offspring of Abraham,
Son of David, and end of exile—who was promised in
Israel's Scriptures and who presented himself as the new
Moses in his teaching and in leading a new exodus for
God's people through his death and resurrection.

INTRODUCTION

AUTHOR   The author did not identify himself in the text. However, the title that ascribes this Gospel to Matthew appears in the earliest manuscripts and is possibly original. Titles became necessary to distinguish one Gospel from another when the four Gospels began to circulate as a single collection. Many early church fathers (Papias, Irenaeus, Pantaenus, and Origen) acknowledged Matthew as the author. Even if Papias was wrong about the original language of the Gospel of Matthew, this does not imply that he and other early church leaders were wrong to identify Matthew as the author of this Gospel. In fact, the early church unanimously affirmed that the Gospel of Matthew was authored by the apostle Matthew. It would require impressive evidence to overturn this early consensus.

BACKGROUND   Determining the date of composition of Matthew's Gospel depends largely on the relationship of the Gospels to one another. Most scholars believe that Matthew utilized Mark's Gospel in writing his own Gospel. If this is correct, Matthew's Gospel must postdate Mark's. However, the date of Mark's Gospel is also shrouded in mystery. Despite Matthew's apparent dependence on Mark, Matthew may have been written any time beginning in the mid-50s once Mark was completed. The earliest historical evidence is consistent with this opinion, since Irenaeus (ca. AD 180) claimed that Matthew wrote his Gospel while Peter and Paul were preaching in Rome (early AD 60s).

MESSAGE AND PURPOSE   Matthew probably wrote his Gospel in order to preserve written eyewitness testimony about the ministry of Jesus. Matthew's Gospel emphasizes certain theological truths. First, Jesus is the Messiah, the long-awaited King of God's people. Second, Jesus is the new Abraham, the founder of a new spiritual Israel consisting of all people who choose to follow him. This new Israel will consist of both Jews and Gentiles. Third, Jesus is the new Moses, the deliverer and instructor of God's people. Fourth, Jesus is the Immanuel, the virgin-born Son of God who fulfills the promises of the Old Testament.

SUMMARY   This Gospel was written from a strong Jewish perspective to show that Jesus is the Messiah promised in the Old Testament.

STRUCTURE   Matthew divided his Gospel into three major sections. He introduced new major sections with the words "from then on Jesus began to" (4:17; 16:21). These transitional statements divide the Gospel into the introduction (1:1–4:16), body (4:17–16:20), and conclusion (16:21–28:20). Matthew also divided his Gospel into five major blocks of teaching, each of which concludes with a summary statement (8:1; 11:1; 13:53; 19:1; 26:1).

Outline

MATTHEW

WORD STUDY

pleroō

Greek pronunciation:
[play RAH oh]

CSB translation:
fulfill

Uses in Matthew: 16
(Mark, 2; Luke, 9; John, 15)
Uses in the NT: 86

Focus passage:
Matthew 8:17

Pleroō (*to fill*) refers to the action of filling up an item with some object (Matt 13:48; Acts 2:2; 5:28) and metaphorically to the filling of persons with certain qualities or powers (Luke 2:40; Acts 2:28; Rom 15:13–14; 2 Tim 1:4) or to the completion (i.e., filling up) of some time period (Mark 1:15; Acts 9:23) or activity (Luke 7:1; Acts 12:25; 13:25). By extension, *pleroō* may also mean *to fulfill* and often indicates the fulfillment of OT prophecies. Prophecies may be directly prophetic (a predicted event is fulfilled; e.g., Jesus's Galilean ministry; Matt 4:13–16; cp. Isa 9:1–2), or they may be indirectly fulfilled by the correspondence of two historical events (the first event foreshadows the second; Matt 27:9; cp. Jer 32:6–9; Zech 11:12–13), or they may be based on parallels between Israel's history and Jesus's life (Israel and Jesus being called out of Egypt; Matt 2:15; cp. Hos 11:1).

stauroō

Greek pronunciation:
[stow RAH oh]

CSB translation:
crucify

Uses in Matthew: 10
(Mark, 8; Luke, 6; John, 11)
Uses in the NT: 46

Focus passage:
Matthew 27:31

Stauroō originally referred to building a fence by driving stakes into the ground. Stakes could easily be used as instruments of death, and impalement became an early form of execution. Through the Roman practice of crucifixion, *stauroō* eventually came to refer primarily to the common form of execution—tying or nailing someone to a cross and leaving them hanging until they died. The vast majority of the occurrences of *stauroō* refer to the manner of Jesus's death, though the NT mentions others who died by *crucifixion* (Matt 23:34; 27:38). Crucifixion was occasionally used as a metaphor for the Christian life (Matt 16:24; Gal 5:24; 6:14), an image emphasizing the believers' identification with Christ and his suffering and death. It thus became a subject of boasting among Christians (Gal 6:14), for their *crucified* Savior was also the risen Lord and Messiah (Acts 2:36; 4:10; 1 Cor 1:23; 2:2; 2 Cor 13:4).

matheteuō

Greek pronunciation:
[mah they TYOO oh]

CSB translation:
make disciples

Uses in Matthew: 3
Uses in the NT: 4

Focus passage:
Matthew 28:19

The verb **matheteuō** (*to make disciples*) is derived from the noun *mathētēs*, which occurs more than 250 times, entirely in the Gospels and Acts. *Mathētēs* means disciple, pupil, one who learns from another and typically indicates a person whose life is bound up with that of Jesus, his master. *Matheteuō* means *to become a disciple* (Matt 13:52; 27:57). In another two occurrences it means *to make disciples* (Matt 28:19; Acts 14:21). In the Great Commission (Matt 28:18–20), the particular Greek construction (aorist participle followed by aorist imperative; this construction is relatively common in Matthew, Luke, and Acts) indicates that the primary weight of Jesus's command in the Great Commission is to *make disciples*, while the act of "going" is a necessary prerequisite to accomplishing this task.

Timeline from Abraham to Jesus

FROM ABRAHAM TO DAVID

2200–1800 BC

2166–1991
Abraham

2066–1886
Isaac

2006–1859
Jacob

1915–1805
Joseph

1526–1000 BC

1526–1406
Moses

1490?–1380?
Joshua

1446
Exodus

1406
Destruction of Jericho

1380?–1060?
Judges

1175?–1125?
Ruth

1105?–1025?
Samuel

1080?–1010
Saul

FROM DAVID TO THE BABYLONIAN EXILE

1000–586 BC

1050?–970
David

990?–931
Solomon

971?–913
Rehoboam

971–909
Jeroboam

722/721
Fall of the northern kingdom

587/586
Fall of the southern kingdom

FROM THE EXILE TO THE MESSIAH

586–63 BC

586–538
Babylonian exile

516
Temple completed

479
Greeks thwart Persian expansion into Europe with victories at Plataea and Mycale.

445
Jerusalem's walls completed

334
Alexander the Great invades Persia.

323–167
Greek control of Palestine

167–63
Years of Jewish independence

63
Roman dominance begins.

THE MESSIAH

5 BC–AD 33

5 BC
Jesus's birth

4 BC
Herod the Great's death

AD 29
John the Baptist's ministry begins.

AD 29
Jesus's ministry begins.

AD 33
Jesus's final week (March 28–April 3)

AD 33
Jesus' resurrection (April 5)

AD 33
Jesus's ascension (May 14)

AD 33
Feast of Pentecost (May 24)

Herod's Family Tree

NAME	FAMILY RELATIONSHIP	REALM OF RESPONSIBILITY	DATES OF REIGN	BIBLICAL REFERENCE
Herod I (the Great)	Son of Antipater	King of Judea	37–4 BC	Matt 2:1–22; Luke 1:5
Herod Archelaus	Oldest son of Herod the Great	Ethnarch of Judea	4 BC–AD 6	Matt 2:2
Philip*	Son of Herod the Great and Cleopatra of Jerusalem	Tetrarch of territories north and east	4 BC–AD 34*	Luke 3:1
Herod Antipas	Youngest son of Herod the Great; second husband of Herodias	Tetrarch of Galilee and Perea	4 BC–AD 39	Matt 14:1–11; Mark 6:14–29; Luke 3:1,19; 13:3–33; 23:7–12
Herod Agrippa I	Grandson of Herod the Great	King of Judea	AD 37–44	Acts 12
Herod Agrippa II	Great-grandson of Herod the Great	Tetrarch and king of Chalcis	AD 44–100 (became king in AD 48)	Acts 25:13–26:32

*Not to be confused with Herod Philip, who was also mentioned in the New Testament. Herod Philip was the son of Herod the Great and Mariamne and was the first husband of Herodias (see Matt 14:3; Mark 6:17; Luke 3:19).

Jesus's Discourses in Matthew

SCRIPTURE	KEY SECTION	NARRATIVE PURPOSE
Matthew 1–4	Opening Narrative	The Introduction
Jesus's Discourses (Sermon Teaching), *Matthew 5–25*	Sermon on the Mount *Matthew 5–7*	The Kingdom Constitution
	Commission of the Twelve *Matthew 10*	The Kingdom's Foundational Leaders
	Kingdom Parables *Matthew 13*	The Pursuit of the Kingdom (in the King's Absence)
	Teaching on the Church *Matthew 18*	The Relational Principles in the Kingdom
	Olivet Discourse *Matthew 24–25*	The Kingdom's Future
Matthew 26–28	Closing Narrative	The Climax

Miracles of Jesus in Matthew

Healing of a Leper	Matt 8:1–4
Healing of the Centurion's Servant	Matt 8:5–13; 7:1–10
Healing of Peter's Mother-in-Law	Matt 8:14–15
Healing of Many Sick	Matt 8:16–17
Calming of the Storm	Matt 8:23–27
Demons Driven Out	Matt 8:28–33
Healing of a Paralytic	Matt 9:1–8
Raising Jairus's Daughter from the Dead	Matt 9:18–26
Healing of the Bleeding Woman	Matt 9:20–22
Healing the Blind	Matt 9:27–31
Healing of a Demon-Possessed Man	Matt 9:32–34
Healing of a Withered Hand	Matt 12:9–14
Healing of a Blind and Mute Man	Matt 12:22–23
Jesus Feeds 5,000	Matt 14:13–21
Walking on Water	Matt 14:22–33
Healing of Many Sick at Gennesaret	Matt 14:34–36
Feeding of the 4,000	Matt 15:32–39
Healing of a Demon-Possessed Boy	Matt 17:14–20
Paying of the Temple Tax	Matt 17:24–27
Healing of the Two Blind Men	Matt 20:29–34
The Barren Fig Tree	Matt 21:18–22

Jewish Sects in
the New Testament

	BELIEF	SELECTED BIBLICAL REFERENCES	ACTIVITIES
PHARISEES	• Monotheistic • Viewed Torah, Prophets, and Writings as authoritative • Accepted both the written and oral law • Focused on keeping of the Sabbath, tithing, and purification rituals • Believed in life after death and the resurrection of the body • Revered humanity and human equality • Missionary-minded toward conversion of Gentiles • Believed individuals were responsible for how they lived	*Matthew 3:7–10; 5:20; 9:14; 16:1,6–12; 22:15–22,34–46; 23:2–36* *Mark 3:6; 7:3–5; 8:15; 12:13–17* *Luke 6:7; 7:36–39; 11:37–44; 18:9–14* *John 3:1; 9:13–16; 11:46–47; 12:19* *Acts 23:6–10* *Philippians 3:4b–6*	• Developers of oral tradition • Taught that the way to God was through obedience to the law • Changed Judaism from a religion of sacrifice to a religion of law • Opposed Jesus because he wouldn't accept the teachings of the oral law as binding • Established and controlled synagogues • Served as religious authorities for most Jews • Emphasized ethical action over theological; legalistic and socially exclusive
SADDUCEES	• Rigidly conservative toward the law • Stressed strict observance of the law • Observed past beliefs and tradition • Opposed oral law as obligatory or binding • Believed that people could do as they wished without attention from God • Denied divine providence, the concept of life after death and the resurrection of the body, and the concept of reward and punishment after death	*2 Samuel 8:17; 15:24* *1 Kings 1:34* *1 Chronicles 12:26–28* *Ezekiel 40:45–46; 43:19; 44:15–16* *Matthew 3:7–10; 16:1,6–12; 22:23–34* *Mark 12:18–27* *Luke 20:27–40* *John 11:47* *Acts 4:1–2; 5:17–18; 23:6–10*	• Politically active • Exercised great political control through the Sanhedrin, of which many were members • Supported the ruling power and the status quo • Leaned toward Hellenism • Opposed both the Pharisees and Jesus • Opposed Jesus for fear their wealth and position would be threatened if they supported him
ZEALOTS	• Similar to the Pharisees with this exception: believed strongly that only God had the right to rule over the Jews; patriotism and religion became inseparable • Believed that total obedience (supported by drastic physical measures) must be apparent before God would bring in the Messianic Age • Were fanatical in their Jewish faith and in their devotion to the law—to the point of martyrdom	*Matthew 10:4* *Mark 3:18* *Luke 6:15* *Acts 1:13*	• Extremely opposed to Roman rule over Palestine and to peace with Rome • Refused to pay taxes • Demonstrated against the use of the Greek language in Palestine • Engaged in terrorism against Rome and others with whom they disagreed politically • Sacarii (or Assassins) were an extremist Zealot group who carried out acts of terrorism against Rome
HERODIANS	• Not a religious group—but a political one • Membership likely comprised of varied theological perspectives	*Matthew 22:5–22* *Mark 3:6; 8:15; 12:13–17*	• Supported Herod and the Herodian dynasty • Accepted Hellenization • Accepted foreign rule

Disciples of Jesus

This chart indicates the order in which each disciple appears in biblical lists.

MATTHEW 10:2–4	MARK 3:16–19	LUKE 6:13–16	ACTS 1:13–14, 26
Simon Peter	Simon Peter	Simon Peter	Peter
Andrew	James the son of Zebedee	Andrew	John
James the son of Zebedee	John	James	James
John	Andrew	John	Andrew
Philip	Philip	Philip	Philip
Bartholomew	Bartholomew	Bartholomew	Thomas
Thomas	Matthew	Matthew	Bartholomew
Matthew the tax collector	Thomas	Thomas	Matthew
James the son of Alphaeus	James the son of Alphaeus	James the son of Alphaeus	James the son of Alphaeus
Thaddaeus	Thaddaeus	Simon who was called the Zealot	Simon the Zealot
Simon the Zealot	Simon the Zealot	Judas the son of James (cp. John 14:22)	Judas the son of James
Judas Iscariot	Judas Iscariot	Judas Iscariot	Matthias, replaced Judas Iscariot (v. 26)

Prophecies Fullfilled by Jesus in Matthew

ASPECTS OF JESUS'S MINISTRY	FULFILLMENT PASSAGE IN MATTHEW	OLD TESTAMENT PROPHECY
His virgin birth and role as God with us	Matt 1:18,22–23	Isa 7:14
His birth in Bethlehem and shepherd role	Matt 2:4–6	Mic 5:2
His refugee years in Egypt and role as God's Son	Matt 2:14–15	Hos 11:1
His upbringing in Nazareth and messianic role (the Hebrew term for *branch* is *nezer*)	Matt 2:23	Isa 11:1
His preaching ministry in Galilee and role as Light to the Gentiles	Matt 4:12–16	Isa 9:1–2
His healing ministry and role as God's Servant	Matt 8:16–17	Isa 53:4
His reluctance to attract attention and his role as God's chosen and loved Servant	Matt 12:16–21	Isa 42:1–4
His teaching in parables and his role in proclaiming God's sovereign rule	Matt 13:34–35	Ps 78:2
His humble entry into Jerusalem and role as King	Matt 21:1–5	Zech 9:9
His betrayal, arrest, and death and role as Suffering Servant	Matt 26:50,56	The prophetic writings as a whole

Hearing the Old Testament in the New

GOD PROMISED A Seed to Abraham *(Gen 12; 15; 17)*

JESUS The Son of Abraham, the Seed *(Matt 1:1; Gal 3:16)*

GOD PROMISED A Descendant on David's Throne Forever *(2 Sam 7)*

JESUS The Son of David, the Son of God *(Matt 1:1; Luke 1:32)*

IMMANUEL A Sign Conceived by a Virgin *(Isa 7:14)*

GOD WITH US The Son Born to Mary, a Virgin *(Matt 1:18–23)*

FROM BETHLEHEM Would Come God's Ruler over Israel *(Mic 5:2)*

IN BETHLEHEM The Messiah Was Born *(Matt 2:1–6; Luke 2:1–6)*

A STAR From Jacob, a Scepter from Israel *(Num 24:17)*

THE KING OF THE JEWS Heralded by a Star *(Matt 2:1–2,9–10)*

ISRAEL God's Son Called out of Egypt *(Exod 5–14; Hos 11:1)*

JESUS God's Son Called out of Egypt *(Matt 2:13–15)*

A VOICE One Crying Out in the Wilderness *(Isa 40:3–5)*

JOHN THE BAPTIST Prepared the Way for the Lord *(Matt 3:1–3)*

GOD'S INSTRUCTION For Israel to Obey *(Deut 6–8)*

GOD'S WORD Fueled Jesus's Obedience *(Matt 4:1–11)*

THE MESSIAH His Mission Proclaimed *(Isa 61:1–2)*

JESUS CHRIST The Scripture Fulfilled *(Luke 4:17–21)*

THE BRONZE SNAKE Lifted Up for the Healing of Those Who Looked *(Num 21:4–9)*

THE SON OF MAN Lifted Up for the Eternal Life of Those Who Believe *(John 3:14–15)*

RESTITUTION BY LAW Repay in Full Plus a Fifth, or a Fourth *(Exod 22:1; Num 5:7)*

RESTITUTION IN GRACE Zacchaeus Repaid Fourfold What He Extorted *(Luke 19:8)*

Christ as a Prophet

A Prophet: Called by God, led by the Spirit of Christ, to deliver the word of the Lord to the people through words and sometimes deeds (*Deut 18:15–9; Luke 24:19; 1 Pet 1:10–12*).

WHO WAS AN OLD TESTAMENT PROPHET?

WORDS	DEEDS
• Proclaimed the word of the Lord • Recorded the word of the Lord • Condemned sin • Warned people of judgment • Called people to repentance • Proclaimed good news • Interpreted present events • Foretold future events	• Performed miracles (healings; even raised the dead) • Acted out a prophetic message

WHO WERE SOME OF THE PROPHETS?

ABRAHAM (*Gen 20:7*)
MOSES (*Deut 18:15–19; 34:10; Acts 7:37*)
SAMUEL (*1 Sam; Acts 13:20*)
DAVID (*Psalms; Acts 2:30*)
NATHAN (*2 Sam 7; 11–12; 1 Kgs 1*)
ELIJAH (*1 Kgs 18:1; Luke 4:25–26*)
ELISHA (*2 Kgs 2:13–15; Luke 4:27*)
JONAH (*2 Kgs 14:25; Jonah 1:1; Matt 12:39*)
ISAIAH (*2 Kgs 19:20; Isa 1:1; Matt 3:3*)
JEREMIAH (*2 Chr 36; Jer 1:2; Matt 2:17*)
EZEKIEL (*Ezek 1:1–3; 2 Cor 6:16*)
ZECHARIAH (*Ezra 6:14; Zech 1:1; Matt 21:4*)

HAGGAI (*Ezra 6:14; Hag 1:1; Heb 12:26*)
DANIEL (*Dan 1:17; Matt 24:15*)
HOSEA (*Hos 1:1; Matt 2:15*)
JOEL (*Joel 1:1; Acts 2:16*)
AMOS (*Amos 1:1–3; Acts 7:42*)
OBADIAH (*Obad 1*)
MICAH (*Mic 1:1; Matt 2:5*)
NAHUM (*Nah 1:1*)
HABAKKUK (*Hab 1:1; Acts 13:40*)
ZEPHANIAH (*Zeph 1:1*)
MALACHI (*Mal 1:1; Matt 11:10*)

HOW WERE THE LORD'S PROPHETS CONFIRMED?
• Their message in the name of the Lord came true
• They did not lead the people to worship other gods

WHAT WAS THE SCOPE OF THEIR MESSAGES?
• Messages primarily delivered to God's people
• Some messages aimed at surrounding nations

HOW WERE THE PROPHETS TREATED?
• Some enjoyed places of prominence and honor
  - Moses was mourned at his death
  - Nathan was an established prophet in David's kingdom
  - Daniel was elevated in the Babylonian and Medo-Persian Empires
• All were persecuted in one way or another
  - Moses was routinely blamed for the people's wandering
  - Elijah was threatened with death
  - Jeremiah was imprisoned

WHO WAS A NEW TESTAMENT PROPHET?

JESUS'S WORDS

- His message: "Repent, because the kingdom of heaven has come near" (*Matt 4:17*)
- He taught in synagogues and preached the good news (*Matt 4:23*)
- He taught as One with authority: "But I tell you you . . ." (*Matt 5:22,28; 7:29*)

JESUS'S DEEDS

- He healed every disease and sickness all over Galilee (*Matt 4:23–24*)
- He raised the widow of Nain's son from the dead (*Luke 7:16*)
- He told the truth of the Samaritan woman's marital history (*John 4:19*)
- He fed the 5,000 from 5 loaves of bread and 2 fish (*John 6:14*)
- He healed a man who had been born blind (*John 9:17*)

WHAT PROPHECIES DID JESUS MAKE?

- His resurrection after three days (*John 2:18–22*)
- His suffering, crucifixion, and resurrection (*Mark 8:31; 9:31; 10:33–34*)
- His raising Lazarus from the dead (*John 11:1–4*)
- The destruction of the temple in Jerusalem (*Matt 24:1–2*)
- Peter's denials of knowing Jesus (*Mark 14:30*)
- His second coming (*John 14:1–3*)

HOW IS JESUS *THE* PROPHET?

- Jesus is the Word who was with God, who was God, and who became flesh (*John 1:1–14*)
- The law was given through Moses; grace and truth through Jesus Christ (*John 1:17*)
- "You have heard that it was said" in the law through Moses; "But I tell you" as Jesus gave the spirit of the law (*Matt 5–7*)
- God spoke through the prophets in the past, but in the last days he has spoken to us by his Son, who reveals God to us (*Heb 1:1–3*)
- "Moses and all the Prophets" testify to Jesus's coming, suffering, crucifixion, and resurrection (*Luke 24:26–27,44–45*)
- Moses wrote about Jesus (*John 5:45–47*)
- Moses had a fading glory after being in God's presence; Jesus is the glory of God (*2 Cor 3*)
- Jesus is the Prophet about whom Moses prophesied the Lord would raise up—to him we must listen (*Acts 3:22*)

HOW WAS JESUS TREATED?

- Some viewed him positively as a prophet of God
  - Some people thought he was John the Baptist, Elijah, Jeremiah, or one of the prophets (*Matt 16:13–14*)
  - Because of his teaching, some thought he was the Prophet (*John 7:40*)
  - The crowds at Jerusalem called him a prophet at his triumphal entry (*Matt 21:11*)
  - The Pharisees were afraid to arrest Jesus because the crowds believed him to be a prophet (*Matt 21:45–46*)
  - The disciples on the road to Emmaus described him as a prophet powerful in word and deed (*Luke 24:19*)
- Others persecuted him as a prophet of God
  - His hometown was offended by him and refused to honor him (*Matt 13:53–58*)
  - The world hated and persecuted him because he revealed the Father to them through his works (*John 15:18–25*)
  - The Pharisees denounced Jesus, saying no prophet arises from Galilee (*John 7:52*)
  - The Sanhedrin took false testimony against him (*Matt 26:59–61*)
  - The Jewish men who arrested him beat him and mocked him as a prophet (*Luke 22:63–65*)
  - His enemies crucified him (*John 19:17–30*)

Long ago, inspired by the Holy Spirit, Moses prophesied of a Prophet to come, One like him to whom God's people should listen. This Prophet would speak God's words and perfectly obey him. The Lord would hold accountable those who do not listen to his Prophet (*Deut 18:15–19*). Jesus alone is the ultimate teacher and has the words of eternal life (*John 6:68*). He is also God's ultimate revelation of himself (*Heb 1:3*). He obeys God's Word; he speaks God's Word; he is God's Word. Jesus is God's Prophet calling us to repentance and faith that we can be saved from our sins and live in peace with Almighty God.

Jesus *Is* God

MATTHEW

PREEXISTENT	• In the beginning the Word was with God, and the Word was God; all of creation was made through him—the Word became flesh (*John 1:1–3,14*) • John the Baptist testified that the One who came after him—Jesus—existed before him (*John 1:14–15*)
THE SON OF GOD	• Conceived in Mary by the Holy Spirit, therefore called the Son of God (*Matt 1:18,20; Luke 1:35*) • The fulfillment of the name "Immanuel," which means "God is with us" (*Matt 1:22–23*) • The voice from heaven proclaimed about Jesus at his baptism: "This is my beloved Son" (*Matt 3:17*) • Inspired by the Father in heaven, Peter proclaimed Jesus is "the Messiah, the Son of the living God" (*Matt 16:15–17*)
WORTHY OF WORSHIP Quoting the Old Testament, Jesus himself said worship should only be given to the Lord God (*Matt 4:10*)	• The wise men worshipped Jesus at his home in Bethlehem and gave him gifts (*Matt 2:9–11*) • Jesus's disciples worshipped him after he walked on the water and came to them in their boat (*Matt 14:33*) • The women at Jesus's tomb worshipped him after seeing his resurrection (*Matt 28:9*) • Jesus's disciples worshipped him on the mountain before his ascension (*Matt 28:17*)
YAHWEH OF THE OLD TESTAMENT	• John the Baptist's mission was to "prepare the way for the Lord," who is Jesus (*Matt 3:1–3; Isa 40:3–5*) • John the Baptist was God's messenger to prepare his way in the person of Jesus (*Matt 11:10; Mal 3:1*)

Hearing the
Old Testament in the New

DAVID'S LORD Called to Sit at the Lord's Right Hand *(Ps 110:1)*	**THE RISEN KING** Ascended into Heaven; Enthroned at God's Right Hand *(Acts 2:34–36)*
THE COMING KING Righteous, Victorious, yet Humble, Riding on a Donkey *(Zech 9:9)*	**THE PROPHESIED KING** Jesus Entered Jerusalem Riding on a Donkey *(Matt 21:1–11)*
THE LORD The Source of Salvation and Blessing *(Ps 118:25–26)*	**THE SON OF DAVID** Praise God for the Salvation and Blessing He Brings *(Matt 21:9)*
THE PSALMIST Suffered for His Zeal for the Lord's House *(Ps 69:9)*	**THE SAVIOR** Cleansed the Temple, Zealous for His Father's House *(John 2:13–22)*
PASSOVER A Lamb's Blood Was Shed to Cover the Israelites' Doorways *(Exod 11–13)*	**THE LORD'S SUPPER** Jesus's Blood Was Shed to Cover the People's Sins *(Matt 26:26–29)*
THE PSALMIST Sang of His Suffering at the Hands of Evildoers *(Ps 22:1–18)*	**JESUS** Cried Out about His Suffering on the Cross *(Matt 27:35–46)*
THE PSALMIST Sang of His Trust in the Lord, the God of Truth *(Ps 31:5)*	**JESUS** Cried Out, Entrusting His Spirit into the Hands of the Father *(Luke 23:46)*
THE PSALMIST Sang of the Lord's Protection over the Bones of the Righteous *(Ps 34:19–20)*	**JESUS** Not One of His Bones Was Broken *(John 19:31–33,36)*
THE LORD They Will Look at Me Whom They Pierced *(Zech 12:10)*	**JESUS** A Soldier Pierced His Side with a Spear, Confirming Death *(John 19:33–34,37)*
JONAH Three Days and Nights in the Belly of the Fish for His Disobedience *(Jonah 1:17)*	**JESUS** Three Days and Nights in the Heart of the Earth for Our Salvation *(Matt 12:40)*
ONE LIKE A SON OF MAN Approached the Ancient of Days on Clouds *(Dan 7:13–14)*	**THE SON OF MAN** Ascended and Will Return on Clouds *(Matt 26:64; Acts 1:9–11)*

Christ as King

A King: Appointed by God as a shepherd for his people, administering justice and leading in the way of righteousness; devotes himself to and delights himself in the law of the Lord and bears witness to the truth for the blessing of God to pour out over his people and into the world *(Deut 17:15–20; Pss 1–2; John 18:36–37).*

WHO WAS AN OLD TESTAMENT KING?

DOS	DON'TS
• Proclaimed the word of the Lord • Recorded the word of the Lord • Condemned sin • Warned people of judgment • Called people to repentance • Proclaimed good news • Interpreted present events • Foretold future events	• Performed miracles (healings; even raised the dead) • Acted out a prophetic message

THE KING . . .	THE KING . . .
• Must write a copy of the law for himself on a scroll in the presence of the priests *(Deut 17:18)* • Must read from his copy of the law every day of his life so he may learn to fear the Lord and observe and obey his instructions and commands *(Deut 17:19)*	• Must not acquire many horses for himself *(Deut 17:16)* • Must not acquire many wives for himself so his heart won't go astray *(Deut 17:17)* • Must not acquire large amounts of silver and gold for himself *(Deut 17:17)* • Must not allow his heart to be exalted above his countrymen *(Deut 17:20)* • Must not turn away from the command of the Lord *(Deut 17:20)*

WHAT RESPONSIBILITIES DID THE KING HAVE?	FROM WHOM DID THE LORD APPOINT HIS KINGS OVER HIS PEOPLE?
• Lead the people to worship and obey the Lord *(Judg 21:25)* • Judge the people, go out before them, and fight their battles *(1 Sam 8:20)*	• Kings would come from Abraham through Sarah *(Gen 17:6,16)* • Kings would come from Jacob *(Gen 35:11)* • Kings would come from Judah *(Gen 49:10)* • Kings would come from David *(2 Sam 7:11–16)*

THE DAVIDIC COVENANT	SOLOMONIC, SON OF DAVID
• The Lord would make a house, a dynasty, for David and raise up his descendant to sit on his throne *(2 Sam 7:11–12)*	• Solomon rode on David's mule to be anointed as king, and then he sat down on David's throne *(1 Kgs 1:32–40)*
• David's descendant would build a house, a temple, for the Lord's name *(2 Sam 7:13)*	• Solomon built the temple for the Lord's name, and the glory of the Lord filled the temple *(1 Kgs 5–8)*
• The Lord would be a father to David's descendant, and he would be a son to the Lord *(2 Sam 7:14)*	• The Lord chose Solomon to be his son, and he would be his Father *(1 Chr 28:6)*
• The Lord would discipline David's descendant but never remove his faithful love from him *(2 Sam 7:14–15)*	• Solomon's many wives turned his heart away to follow other gods, so the Lord took away the peace of the kingdom and sent enemies against Solomon; he also took the kingdom away from Solomon's son, leaving only one tribe to him for the sake of David *(1 Kgs 11)*
• David's house and kingdom will endure forever, and his throne will be established forever *(2 Sam 7:16)*	• Solomon failed to persevere in keeping the Lord's commands, so his kingdom was not established forever *(1 Chr 28:7)*

HOW WAS JESUS KING?

HE WAS A DESCENDANT OF . . .

Abraham	**Jacob**	**Judah**	**David**
Matthew 1:1–2,17	Matthew 1:2	Matthew 1:2–3	Matthew 1:1,6,17
Luke 3:34	Luke 3:34	Luke 3:33	Luke 3:31

DOS

THE KING . . .	JESUS . . .
• Must write a copy of the law for himself on a scroll in the presence of the priests *(Deut 17:18)*	• Taught with authority, giving the full meaning of the law and fulfilling the Law and the Prophets *(Matt 5–7)*
• Must read from his copy of the law every day of his life so he may learn to fear the Lord and observe and obey his instructions and commands *(Deut 17:19)*	• Had the law written on his heart, quoting from it to fight temptation from the devil *(Matt 4:1–11)*

DON'TS

THE KING . . .	JESUS . . .
• Must not acquire many horses for himself *(Deut 17:16)*	• Borrowed a donkey and her foal for his "triumphal entry" into Jerusalem *(Matt 21:1–11)*
• Must not acquire many wives for himself so his heart won't go astray *(Deut 17:17)*	• Has one bride—the church *(Rev 21)*
• Must not acquire large amounts of silver and gold for himself *(Deut 17:17)*	• Had no place to lay his head *(Matt 8:20)*
• Must not allow his heart to be exalted above his countrymen *(Deut 17:20)*	• Washed his disciples' feet as an example of his servant heart *(John 13:1–17)*
• Must not turn away from the command of the Lord *(Deut 17:20)*	• Was tempted in every way as we are, yet without sin *(Heb 4:15)*

HOW IS JESUS *THE* KING?

THE DAVIDIC COVENANT	JESUS, *THE* SON OF DAVID
• The Lord would make a house, a dynasty, for David and raise up his descendant to sit on his throne *(2 Sam 7:11–12)*	• Jesus is the promised Son of David, the Messiah-King *(Matt 1:1–17)*
• David's descendant would build a house, a temple, for the Lord's name *(2 Sam 7:13)*	• Jesus cleansed the temple in his zeal for the Lord's holiness, but even more so, he declared himself to be the temple of God, raised up in three days *(John 2:13–22)*
• The Lord would be a father to David's descendant, and he would be a son to the Lord *(2 Sam 7:14)*	• Jesus is the beloved Son of God *(Matt 3:16–17; 17:5; Luke 1:30–33; Heb 1:5)*
• The Lord would discipline David's descendant but never remove his faithful love from him *(2 Sam 7:14–15)*	• Jesus is the Good Shepherd who laid down his life for his sheep, saving them from their sin so they will never lose God's faithful love *(Matt 26:26–29; John 10:11–18,27–30)*
• David's house and kingdom will endure forever, and his throne will be established forever *(2 Sam 7:16)*	• Jesus has received all authority in heaven and on earth, and he will be with his disciples always, to the end of the age *(Matt 28:18–20; Luke 1:32–33)*

From the beginning, God has expected his created image bearers to rule over the created order. But sin brought exile from the first garden kingdom and separation from the supreme King over the world, resulting in suffering, hardship, and injustice. As God promised Abraham and David, one day a holy and righteous King—Jesus—would come to set everything right. The Son of God's perfect obedience and sacrificial death in his first coming were vindicated in his resurrection, and he has received all authority in heaven and on earth. So from his throne at the right hand of the Father, he pours out the Holy Spirit on his ambassadors to proclaim the gospel of the kingdom until his enemies are made his footstool *(Ps 110:1)*. The crucified and resurrected King has won the victory over sin and death, so his peace reigns over his followers, and at his second coming his peace will rest over all of creation.

Jesus's Suffering

According to the Old Testament Scriptures—Moses and all the Prophets—
the Messiah had to suffer these things and enter into his glory (*Luke 24:26–27*).

JESUS'S SUFFERING	OLD TESTAMENT TYPES AND PROPHECIES	JESUS'S FOLLOWERS WILL SUFFER	FOLLOW JESUS'S EXAMPLE AND COMMANDS
JESUS WAS TEMPTED (MATT 4:1–11; HEB 2:18)	• The first Adam was tempted (*Gen 3:1–7*) • Israel was tested in the wilderness (*Numbers–Deuteronomy*)	• Temptation is common to all humanity, both from without and from within (*1 Cor 10:1–13; Jas 1:14–15*)	• Trust that God is faithful, and so escape, endure, and flee from idolatry (*1 Cor 10:13–14*) • Quote Scripture in context (*Matt 4:4,7,10*)
JESUS WAS BETRAYED (MATT 26:14–16,47–50; LUKE 24:7; JOHN 13:18; ACTS 1:16)	• A friend betrays (*Ps 41:9*) • 30 pieces of silver as a price (*Zech 11:12–13*)	• Betrayal by family and friends as those who hate Christ (*Luke 21:16–17*)	• Rejoice as you share in the sufferings of Christ and entrust yourself to a faithful Creator while continuing to do good (*1 Pet 4:13–19*)
JESUS FELT THE WEIGHT OF THE CUP OF GOD'S WRATH (MATT 26:36–44)	• The Lord's cup for the wicked (*Ps 75:8*) • The cup of the Lord's wrath (*Isa 51:17–20*) • The cup of wrath for the nations (*Jer 25:15–29*)	— [There is no condemnation for those who are in Christ Jesus (*Rom 8:1*)]	—
BY HIS DISCIPLES (MATT 26:31,56) **AND DENIED BY PETER** (MATT 26:69–75)	• Strike the shepherd and the sheep are scattered (*Zech 13:7*)	• Brothers and sisters in Christ might sin against each other (*Matt 18:15*)	• Seek repentance, reconciliation, and restoration and forgive (*Matt 18:15–22; John 21:15–19*)
JESUS WAS MOCKED, BEATEN, AND FALSELY ACCUSED (MATT 26:57–68; 27:27–31,36–44)	• The Suffering Servant was despised and rejected, oppressed and afflicted (*Isa 53:3,7*) • The psalmist was scorned, despised, and mocked (*Ps 22:6–8*)	• Suffering and persecution at the hands of the world on account of Jesus's name (*Matt 5:10–11; John 15:20–21; 16:33*)	• Rejoice and have courage (*Matt 5:12; John 16:33*) • Do not return insults and do not threaten, but entrust yourself to the One who judges justly (*1 Pet 2:21–23*)
JESUS WAS CRUCIFIED AND DRANK THE CUP OF GOD'S WRATH IN OUR PLACE (MATT 27:33–50; JOHN 19:16–37)	• The Passover (*Exod 11–13*), reinstituted in the Lord's Supper—the bread (Jesus's broken body) and the cup of the new covenant (Jesus's shed blood) • The psalmist felt abandoned by God (*Ps 22:1*) • Pierced hands and feet (*Ps 22:14–18*) • The Suffering Servant pierced for others' rebellion (*Isa 53:5*) • It pleased the Lord to crush the Servant severely as an offering of atonement (*Isa 53:10*) • Look upon the One whom they pierced (*Zech 12:10*)	— [God made him who had no sin to be sin for us so we might become the righteousness of God in him (*2 Cor 5:21*)]	—

Parables of the Kingdom

THE PARABLE	REFERENCE(S)	SOME DETAILS	KINGDOM SIGNIFICANCE
THE SOWER AND THE SOILS	Matthew 13:1–9,18–23; Mark 4:1–9,13–20; Luke 8:4–8,11–15	• Explanation given in Scripture • Specific allegorical interpretation	The word about the kingdom—the gospel—is fruitful only in a heart that hears and understands the good news, yet the message must still be shared like the indiscriminate casting of seed on the ground
THE WHEAT AND THE WEEDS	Matthew 13:24–30, 36–43	• Explanation given in Scripture • Specific allegorical interpretation	The Father's kingdom will come in its fullness at the end of the age when the unrighteous "children of the evil one" will be judged and condemned to hell and the righteous "children of the kingdom" will be glorified and blessed in the kingdom
THE MUSTARD SEED/THE YEAST	Matthew 13:31–33; Luke 13:18–21 (see also Mark 4:30–32)	• Two parables with similar meanings	The kingdom will start small but will have a very large impact upon the world, permeating it in its entirety
THE HIDDEN TREASURE AND THE PRICELESS PEARL	Matthew 13:44–46	• Two parables with similar meanings	The kingdom is of such value that it is worth sacrificing everything we have in order to be a part of it
THE UNMERCIFUL SERVANT	Matthew 18:21–35	• An extended story • Told in response to Peter's question about forgiving others	The kingdom is comprised of people who forgive others from their heart because they recognize the infinite extent to which God has forgiven them
THE WICKED TENANTS	Matthew 21:33–46; Mark 12:1–12; Luke 20:9–19	• Specific allegorical interpretation • Pharisees recognized this parable was spoken against them	The kingdom is comprised of people who produce its fruit; failure to produce fruit for God, exemplified in the rejection of his Son, Jesus, is to reject participation in the kingdom of God
THE GOOD SAMARITAN	Luke 10:25–37	• An extended story • Told in response to an expert in the law's question about eternal life and "Who is my neighbor?"	The kingdom is comprised of those who see themselves as neighbors without boundaries and who show mercy to others
THE LOST AND FOUND PARABLES	Luke 15	• Three parables with similar meanings • Told in response to complaints from the Pharisees and teachers of the law that Jesus would welcome and eat with sinners	
•THE LOST SHEEP/LOST COIN	Luke 15:1–10	• Two short parables about something of value being lost and then found	The kingdom of heaven rejoices over even one sinner who repents
•THE LOST SON(S)	Luke 15:11–32	• An extended story • Some allegorical interpretation • Just as much significance in the older brother who stayed as in the prodigal younger brother who returned	The kingdom of heaven rejoices over a sinner who repents; refusal to rejoice over a sinner's repentance is to find oneself on the outside of the kingdom
THE PHARISEE AND THE TAX COLLECTOR	Luke 18:9–14	• A short parable • Told in response to some who trusted in their own righteousness and looked down on others	The kingdom is comprised of those who humble themselves before God and rely solely upon God's mercy for their salvation; these will be exalted, but those who exalt themselves will be humbled

Mark

Genre | **GOSPEL, HISTORICAL NARRATIVE**

Jesus is the enigmatic Messiah and Son of God who is leading the people of God in an exodus into a new stage of God's kingdom, as evidenced by his teachings, healings, and exorcisms and confirmed by his death and resurrection.

INTRODUCTION

AUTHOR   The Gospel of Mark is anonymous. Eusebius, the early church historian, writing in AD 326, preserved the words of Papias, an early church father. Papias quoted "the elder," probably John, as saying that Mark recorded Peter's preaching about the things Jesus said and did, but not in order. Thus Mark was considered the author of this Gospel even in the first century.

BACKGROUND   According to the early church fathers, Mark wrote his Gospel in Rome just before or just after Peter's martyrdom. Further confirmation of the Roman origin of Mark's Gospel is found in Mark 15:21, where Mark noted that Simon, a Cyrenian who carried Jesus's cross, was the father of Alexander and Rufus, men apparently known to the believers in Rome. Most Bible scholars are convinced that Mark was the earliest Gospel and served as one of the sources for Matthew and Luke.

MESSAGE AND PURPOSE   Mark's Gospel is a narrative about Jesus. Mark identifies his theme in the first verse: "the gospel of Jesus Christ, the Son of God." That Jesus is the divine Son of God is the major emphasis of his Gospel. God announced it at Jesus's baptism in 1:11. Demons and unclean spirits recognized and acknowledged it in 3:11 and 5:7. God reaffirmed it at the transfiguration in 9:7. Jesus taught it parabolically in 12:1–12, hinted at it in 13:32, and confessed it directly in 14:61–62. Finally, the Roman centurion confessed it openly and without qualification in 15:39. Thus Mark's purpose was to summon people to repent and respond in faith to the good news of Jesus Christ, the Son of God (1:1,15).

SUMMARY   Mark's Gospel emphasizes actions and deeds. Jesus is on the go—healing, casting out demons, performing miracles, hurrying from place to place, and teaching. In Mark everything happens "immediately." As soon as one episode ends, another begins. The rapid pace slows down when Jesus enters Jerusalem (11:1). Thereafter, events are marked by days, and his final day by hours.

STRUCTURE   Mark's Gospel begins with a Prologue (1:1–13), which is then followed by three major sections. The first (1:14–8:21) tells of Jesus's Galilean ministry. There Jesus healed and cast out demons and worked miracles. The second section (8:22–10:52) is transitional. Jesus began his journey that would take him to Jerusalem. The final section (11:1–16:8) involves a week in Jerusalem. From the time Jesus entered the city he was at odds with the religious leaders, who quickly brought about his execution. A brief appendix (16:9–20) records some of Jesus's appearances, his commissioning of his disciples, and his ascension.

Outline

WORD STUDY

apostolos

Greek pronunciation:
[ah PAHSS tah lahss]

CSB translation:
apostle

Uses in Mark's Gospel: 2
Uses in the NT: 80

Focus passage: Mark 3:14

The Greek noun *apostolos* comes from the common verb *apostellō* and literally means "one sent forth with a message." The noun did not attain the significance of being sent with authority until its adoption by Jesus and the NT writers. The original twelve disciples were chosen and named *apostles* by Jesus (Matt 10:2; Mark 3:14; Luke 6:13); they were trained by him (see Acts 1:15–26) and were invested with his authority to lead the church to accomplish the task he gave it (Matt 28:18–20). Apostles had to be eyewitnesses of Jesus's resurrection (Acts 1:22; 1 Cor 9:1; 15:8–9). Together with prophets, apostles were foundational for the early church (Eph 2:20), particularly in being responsible for giving divine revelation to God's people (Eph 3:5). Only 15 people are clearly referred to as *apostles* in the NT: the original Twelve, Matthias (Acts 1:26), Paul, and Barnabas (Acts 14:14).

sōzō

Greek pronunciation:
[SOH zoh]

CSB translation:
save

Uses in Mark's Gospel: 15
Uses in the NT: 106

Focus passage:
Mark 13:13

The Greek verb *sōzō* literally means "to preserve" or "to keep safe" with an underlying idea of "making whole." The term can refer to saving someone from physical harm (Matt 8:25) or death (Matt 14:30; 15:30–31; Acts 27:20,31), healing (Mark 5:23,28; 6:56), exorcism (Luke 8:36), or deliverance from a severe ordeal (John 12:27; Heb 5:7; Jude 5). The most common use of *sōzō* in the NT, especially in Acts and the Epistles, is to describe the various aspects of salvation. Two important nouns are derived from *sōzō*: (1) *sotēria*, which means salvation (in the redemptive sense) or *deliverance* from physical death or danger (see Acts 7:25; 27:34); (2) *sotēr*, which means "Savior" and is always a reference to either the Father or Jesus Christ in the work of redemption.

enkataleipō

Greek pronunciation:
[en kah tah LAY poh]

CSB translation:
abandon

Uses in Mark's Gospel: 1
Uses in the NT: 10

Focus passage:
Mark 15:34

The Greek verb *enkataleipō* is a double compound that produces an intensive form of a verb meaning "to lack or leave" (*leipō*). With one exception (Rom 9:29), each occurrence of the term in the NT means "forsake" or "abandon." In Mark 15:34 and Matthew 27:46, *enkataleipō* is used to translate the Aramaic word *sabach*, which in turn translates the original Hebrew *'azab* in Psalm 22:1. Jesus's quoting of this verse occurred toward the end of three hours of darkness (Mark 15:33) during which he endured God's wrath by being separated from the Father as payment for the sins of mankind. The word *enkataleipō* also occurs in Hebrews 13:5: "I will never . . . abandon you." Since this promise is addressed to believers, it indicates that while God was willing to *abandon* Jesus on the cross in order to redeem us, he is not now willing to *abandon* those whom he has redeemed.

Mark Timeline

75–50 BC

73
The Hittites destroy Babylon.

63
Pompey conquers Jerusalem.

58–51
Rome's Gallic wars begin after Julius Caesar becomes Roman governor of Gaul.

55
Pompey builds first stone amphitheater in Rome.

55–54
Julius Caesar invades Britain.

50 BC–AD 9

50
Circus Maximus is built in Rome.

44
Mark Antony controls Rome; Julius Caesar is assassinated.

40–37
Parthians conquer Jerusalem.

37
Herod becomes "king of the Jews."

31
Qumran is abandoned as a result of an earthquake in the vicinity of Jericho.

27
Octavian becomes Augustus Caesar.

AD 9–30

9
Jesus visits the temple at the age of 12.

14–37
Tiberius, Rome's second emperor

18–36
Caiaphas, Jewish high priest

29
Jesus is baptized and begins calling disciples.

29–30
Jesus's early ministry in Judea (John 2–4)

AD 30–33

30–32
Jesus's Galilean ministry (all four Gospels)

32
Jesus travels with disciples and engages in intensive training (Matthew, Mark, and Luke).

32
Jesus's later ministry in Judea (Luke and John)

33
Jesus's Perean ministry (Luke and John)

33
Jesus's crucifixion, resurrection, exaltation (all four Gospels)

Places in Jesus's Ministry

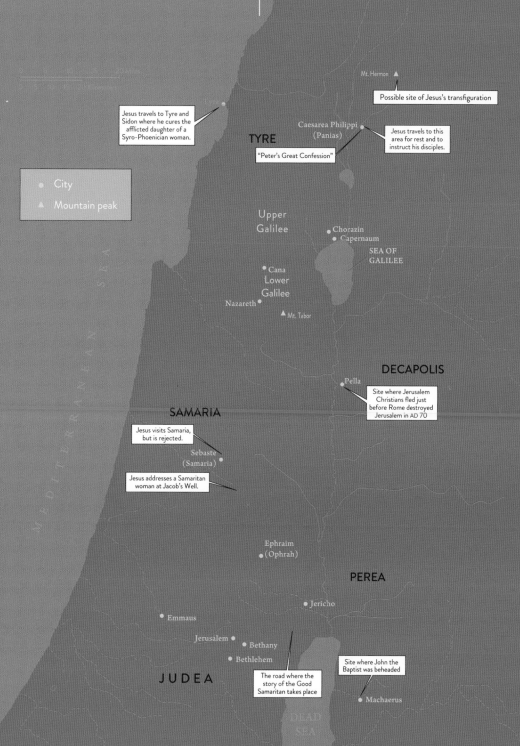

Mt. Hermon ▲

Possible site of Jesus's transfiguration

Jesus travels to Tyre and Sidon where he cures the afflicted daughter of a Syro-Phoenician woman.

Caesarea Philippi (Panias)

Jesus travels to this area for rest and to instruct his disciples.

TYRE

"Peter's Great Confession"

- City
▲ Mountain peak

Upper Galilee

Chorazin
Capernaum

SEA OF GALILEE

Cana

Lower Galilee

Nazareth

▲ Mt. Tabor

DECAPOLIS

Pella

Site where Jerusalem Christians fled just before Rome destroyed Jerusalem in AD 70

SAMARIA

Jesus visits Samaria, but is rejected.

Sebaste (Samaria)

Jesus addresses a Samaritan woman at Jacob's Well.

MEDITERRANEAN SEA

Ephraim (Ophrah)

PEREA

Jericho

Emmaus

Jerusalem
Bethany
Bethlehem

Site where John the Baptist was beheaded

JUDEA

The road where the story of the Good Samaritan takes place

Machaerus

DEAD SEA

Passion Week

O **SATURDAY**
- Jesus anointed by Mary at Bethany (John 12:1–8; cp. Matt 26:6–13)

O **SUNDAY**
- Jesus's "triumphal entry" into Jerusalem on a donkey (Matt 21:1–11; Mark 11:1–11; Luke 19:28–40; John 12:12–18)
  - *Jesus wept over Jerusalem (Luke 19:41–44)*

O **MONDAY**
- Jesus cleansed the temple of money changers and those selling doves (Matt 21:12–13; Mark 11:15–17; Luke 19:45–46; cp. John 2:13–22)

O **TUESDAY**
- Jesus taught in the temple (Matt 21:23–23:39; Mark 11:27–12:44; Luke 20:1–21:4)
  - *Jesus wisely answered the entrapments of the Jewish leaders in the temple*
  - *Jesus lamented over Jerusalem's rejection of God's will*
- Jesus predicted the destruction of the temple and then taught the disciples about the signs of the end of the age on the Mount of Olives (Matt 24:1–25:46; Mark 13:1–37; Luke 21:5–36)

O **THURSDAY**
- Jesus celebrated the Passover with his disciples (Matt 26:20–35; Mark 14:17–26; Luke 22:14–38)
  - *Jesus washed the disciples' feet (John 13:1–20)*
  - *Jesus reinstituted the Passover as the Lord's Supper, which now proclaims his sacrificial death*
  - *Jesus taught his disciples in the upper room and prayed (John 13:31–17:26)*
- Jesus predicted Peter's denials and the disciples' abandoning him (Matt 26:31–35; Mark 14:27–31; Luke 22:31–34)
- Jesus was deeply troubled as he prayed in Gethsemane for the cup of God's wrath to pass from him, but he committed himself to the Father's will (Matt 26:36–46; Mark 14:32–42; Luke 22:39–46)
- Jesus was betrayed by Judas and arrested (Matt 26:47–6; Mark 14:43–52; Luke 22:47–53; John 18:1–12)

O **FRIDAY**
Jesus was put on trial before Annas, Caiaphas the high priest, and the Sanhedrin (Matt 26:57–75; Mark 14:53–72; Luke 22:54–71; John 18:13–27)
  - *Peter denied Jesus three times*
- Jesus was put on trial before Pilate (Matt 27:1–2, 11–14; Mark 15:1–5; Luke 23:1–5; John 18:28–38)
  - *Judas hanged himself (Matt 27:3–10)*
- Jesus was taken before Herod (Luke 23:6–12)
- Jesus was taken back to Pilate (Matt 27:15–26; Mark 15:6–15; Luke 23:13–25; John 18:38–19:16)
  - *Barabbas was released*
- Jesus was mocked as a king and then crucified as "the King of the Jews" (Matt 27:27–56; Mark 15:16–41; Luke 23:26–49; John 19:16–37)
  - *Jesus cried out, feeling abandoned by the Father*
  - *Jesus cried out, entrusting his spirit to the Father*
- Jesus was buried (Matt 27:57–66; Mark 15:42–47; Luke 23:50–56; John 19:38–42)

O **SUNDAY**
- Jesus rose from the dead and appeared to some of his followers (Matt 28:1–10; Mark 16:1–8; Luke 24:1–49; John 20:1–23)
  - *To the women leaving the empty tomb (Matt 28:9–10; cp. John 20:11–18)*
  - *To Simon Peter (Luke 24:34)*
  - *To the two disciples on the road to Emmaus (Luke 24:13–31)*
  - *To the disciples (without Thomas) in a locked room in Jerusalem (Luke 24:36–49; John 20:19–23)*

Cross Connections

PSALM 22	MARK 15
"My God, my God, why have you forsaken me?" *(Ps 22:1)*	Jesus cried out with a loud voice, . . . "My God, my God, why have you abandoned me?" *(Mark 15:34)*
"Everyone who sees me mocks me; they sneer and shake their heads" *(Ps 22:7)*	• Passersby insulted Jesus on the cross and shook their heads *(Mark 15:29)* • Chief priests and scribes mocked Jesus on the cross *(Mark 15:31)* • The two criminals crucified with Jesus taunted him *(Mark 15:32)*
"He relies on the Lᴏʀᴅ; let him save him" *(Ps 22:8)*	Passersby, chief priests, and scribes taunted Jesus to "save himself" *(Mark 15:29–32)*
"Many bulls surround me. . . . They open their mouths against me. . . . Dogs have surrounded me; a gang of evildoers has closed in on me" *(Ps 22:12–13,16)*	• The crowd of Jews shouted, "Crucify him!" *(Mark 15:11–14)* • A whole company of Roman soldiers gathered to mock Jesus and then crucify him *(Mark 15:16–20)*
"You put me into the dust of death" *(Ps 22:15)*	Jesus died on the cross and was buried in a tomb *(Mark 15:37,42–46)*
"They pierced my hands and my feet" *(Ps 22:16)*	Jesus was crucified *(Mark 15:24–25)*
"They divided my garments among themselves, and they cast lots for my clothing" *(Ps 22:18)*	Roman soldiers divided Jesus's garments and then cast lots to see who would get them *(Mark 15:24)*

MARK

Hearing the
Old Testament in the New

THE GREAT I AM God Alone Treads upon the Waves of the Sea *(Job 9:8)*	**JESUS, THE SON OF GOD** The I AM Who Walked on the Sea *(Matt 14:25–27)*
ISAIAH'S MESSAGE Listen, but Not Understand; See, but Not Perceive *(Isa 6:9–10)*	**JESUS'S PARABLES** Understanding Given to the Kingdom's Disciples *(Mark 4:11–12)*
THE PSALMIST'S PROPHECY My People Listen to the Speaker of Parables *(Ps 78:1–3)*	**THE PROPHECY'S FULFILLMENT** Jesus Spoke to the Crowd in Parables *(Matt 13:34–35)*
GOD'S LAW Love the Lord; Love Your Neighbor *(Deut 6:5; Lev 19:18)*	**JESUS'S AFFIRMATION** Obey the Law Completely to Inherit Eternal Life *(Luke 10:25–28)*
THE HYPOCRITES Honor God with Lips, but Hearts Are Far from Him *(Isa 29:13–14)*	**THE PHARISEES** Teach as Doctrines the Commands of Men *(Mark 7:6–7)*
THE LORD'S VINEYARD God's People Returned Wicked Fruit *(Isa 5:1–7)*	**JESUS'S PARABLE** The Pharisees Would Kill the Lord's Son *(Matt 21:33–46)*
THE REJECTED STONE Rejected by the Builders but Became the Cornerstone *(Ps 118:22–24)*	**THE REJECTED SAVIOR** Rejected by the Wicked, Given to the Fruitful *(Matt 21:42–46)*
THE JUDGMENT God's Enemies Will Feed the Worm and Fuel the Fire Forever *(Isa 66:24)*	**JESUS'S WARNING** Hell, Described as the Place of the Worm and Fire *(Mark 9:47–48)*
MOSES Prepared the People to Receive God's Manna *(Exod 16)*	**JESUS** Gave the 5,000 Bread; He Is the Bread of Life *(Matt 14:19–20; John 6:32–35)*
THE LORD'S DESIRE Steadfast Love and Not Sacrifice *(Hos 6:6)*	**JESUS'S MISSION** To Heal the Spiritually Sick and Give Mercy to Sinners *(Matt 9:1–13)*
THE SUFFERING SERVANT Bore Our Sufferings; Carried Our Sorrows *(Isa 53:4)*	**JESUS** Cast Out Spirits with a Word; Healed All Who Were Sick *(Matt 8:16–17)*

Jesus's Miracles

MIRACLE	WITNESSES	PURPOSE	RESULT
JESUS WALKED ON WATER (MATT 14:22–33; SEE ALSO MARK 6:45–52; JOHN 6:16–21)	The disciples	Demonstrated Jesus's identity as "I AM" (*Matt 14:27*)	The disciples worshipped Jesus as the Son of God (*Matt 14:33*)
JESUS HEALED A BLIND MAN (MARK 10:46–52; SEE ALSO MATT 20:29–34; LUKE 18:35–43)	The disciples, Bartimaeus, and a large crowd from Jericho	Demonstrated Jesus's ability to give sight to the blind as the Messiah, the Son of God (*Mark 1:1; 10:48,51-52*)	The formerly blind man began to follow Jesus on the road (*Mark 10:52*)
JESUS CAST OUT DEMONS (LUKE 8:26–39; SEE ALSO MATT 8:28–34; MARK 5:1–20)	The disciples, the man who had been demon-possessed, and all the people of the Gerasene region	Demonstrated Jesus's authority over evil and the spiritual realm as the Son of the Most High God (*Luke 8:28-33*)	The people of the region asked Jesus to leave, but the man who had been demon-possessed told others about everything Jesus had done for him (*Luke 8:37-39*)
JESUS HEALED A MAN WHO HAD A DISABILITY FOR 38 YEARS (JOHN 5:1–16)	The man who was healed of his disability, and later some of the Jews who objected to him carrying his mat on the Sabbath	Demonstrated Jesus's unity with the Father and authority over the Sabbath (*John 5:17-23*)	The Jews began persecuting Jesus because he healed and encouraged "work" on the Sabbath and made himself equal to God by calling God his Father (*John 5:16,18*)
JESUS FED THE 5,000 (JOHN 6:1–15; SEE ALSO MATT 14:13–21; MARK 6:30–44; LUKE 9:10–17)	The disciples and the crowd of 5,000 men	Demonstrated Jesus is greater than Moses; Jesus is the bread of life and the Son of God (*John 6:26-69*)	The crowd rejected Jesus's teaching, but the disciples believed he is the Holy One of God (*John 6:66-69*)

Jesus's Ministry

City ●
Mountain peak ▲
Administrative capital ★

Possible site of Jesus's transfiguration

Mt. Hermon ▲

● Caesarea Philippi (Panias)

Traditional site of
Sermon on the Mount

Jesus fed the 5,000.

Jesus walked
on water.

Capernaum ●

Cana ●

SEA OF
GALILEE

● Nazareth

● Gadara

The region of the Gerasenes,
where Jesus delivered the
Gadarene demoniac

★ Caesarea Maritima
(Strato's Tower)

M E D I T E R R A N E A N   S E A

Joppa ●

Jericho ●

Jerusalem ● Bethany

Jesus taught about
the Good Shepherd.

Jesus's Ministry in Jerusalem

Gate

Tower

Wall

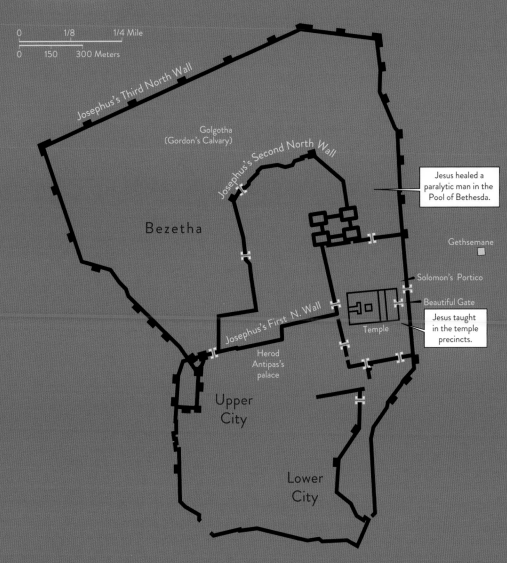

0   1/8   1/4 Mile

0   150   300 Meters

Josephus's Third North Wall

Golgotha
(Gordon's Calvary)

Josephus's Second North Wall

Bezetha

Jesus healed a
paralytic man in the
Pool of Bethesda.

Gethsemane

Solomon's Portico

Beautiful Gate

Josephus's First N. Wall

Jesus taught
in the temple
precincts.

Temple

Herod
Antipas's
palace

Upper
City

Lower
City

Luke

Genre | GOSPEL, HISTORICAL NARRATIVE

Jesus came as the Spirit-anointed Suffering Servant and
Son of Man to seek and save the lost through his life,
death, resurrection, and ascension, revealing the
unexpected nature of God's kingdom
and its inclusion of repentant sinners of all sorts.

INTRODUCTION

AUTHOR   The author of the Third Gospel is not named. Considerable evidence points to Luke as its author. Much of that proof is found in the book of Acts, which identifies itself as a sequel to Luke (Acts 1:1–3). A major line of evidence has to do with the "we" sections of the book (Acts 16:10–17; 20:5–15; 21:1–18; 27:1–37; 28:1–16). Most of Acts is narrated in third-person plural ("they," "them"), but some later sections having to do with the ministry of the apostle Paul unexpectedly shift to first-person plural ("we," "us"). Among Paul's well-known coworkers, the most likely candidate is Luke, the doctor (see Col 4:14; Phlm 24).

BACKGROUND   Traditionally, the Gospel of Luke is believed to have been written after both Matthew and Mark. Those who date Matthew and Mark in the AD 60s or 70s have tended to push the dating of Luke back to the AD 70s or 80s. The Third Gospel is addressed to "most honorable Theophilus" (Luke 1:3), about whom nothing else is known other than that he is also the recipient of the book of Acts (Acts 1:1). The title "most honorable" indicates that, at the least, he was a person of high standing and financial substance. It may also reflect that he was an official with some governmental authority and power.

MESSAGE AND PURPOSE   The Gospel of Luke is a carefully researched (1:3), selective presentation of the person and life of Jesus Christ, designed to strengthen the faith of believers (1:3–4) and to challenge the misconceptions of unbelievers, especially those from a Greek background. Its portrait of Jesus is well-balanced, skillfully emphasizing his divinity and perfect humanity.

SUMMARY   The Gospel of Luke is the longest book in the New Testament. Focusing on the life and ministry of Jesus Christ, this Gospel is part one of a two-part history, the book of Acts being part two. Both were dedicated to "most honorable Theophilus" (Luke 1:3; Acts 1:1).

STRUCTURE   Luke's distinctive "narrative about the events" (1:1) of the life of Jesus is written in "orderly sequence" (1:3), though not strict chronological sequence in many cases (as the notes will explain at various points). Generally, after the key events leading up to the beginning of Christ's public ministry (1:5–4:13), the flow of the book is from his early ministry in and around Galilee (4:14–9:50), through an extended description of ministry related to his journey to Jerusalem (9:51–19:44), climaxing in the events of Passion Week and postresurrection appearances in and around Jerusalem (19:45–24:53).

Outline

parthenos

Greek pronunciation:
[pahr THEHN ahss]

CSB translation:
virgin

Uses in Luke's Gospel: 2
Uses in the NT: 15

Focus passage:
Luke 1:27,34

In the Greek NT, *parthenos* (virgin) connotes an unmarried female virgin of marriageable age. Once, the term refers to a male *virgin* (Rev 14:4). Both Matthew and Luke acknowledge that Mary was a *parthenos* at the time she conceived Jesus (Matt 1:20,23; Luke 1:27,34), and Matthew indicates that she remained a virgin while she carried the child to term (Matt 1:25). Both books mention the salvific significance of Jesus's birth (Matt 1:21; Luke 1:31–32). However, Matthew alone indicates the prophetic significance of Jesus's birth by a *virgin* (Matt 1:23). According to Matthew, Mary was the fulfillment of a prophecy given through the prophet Isaiah, who described a *virgin* (Isa 7:14; *parthenos* occurs here in the Greek OT) who would give birth to a child to be named Immanuel. Matthew applies this prophecy to Christ's birth.

paradeisos

Greek pronunciation:
[pah RAH day sahss]

CSB translation:
paradise

Uses in Luke's Gospel: 1
Uses in the NT: 3

Focus passage:
Luke 23:43

The word "paradise" in Luke 23:43 is transliterated directly from the Greek word *paradeisos*, which occurs in only two other places in the NT. In the Greek world *paradeisos* could refer to a garden, a grove, or a park; thus, it is the word found in the Greek OT for the garden of Eden (11 times in Gen 2–3). Luke 23:43 and 2 Corinthians 12:4 use *paradeisos* to refer to the place where God especially manifests his presence, which we call heaven. Revelation 2:7 refers to *paradeisos* as the place where believers (those who "conquer") eat from "the tree of life," which is in the new Jerusalem (see Rev 22:2,14,19).

LUKE

First-Century Roman World

LUKE

Rome

Puteoli ITALIA

Malta

ADRIATIC SEA

MACEDONIA

Berea
Thessalonica

CYRENAICA

Cyrene

MEDITERRANEAN SEA

ACHAIA

Sparta

Athens

Neapolis

THRACE

Byzantium
(Istanbul)

AEGEAN SEA

Crete

Ephesus

Pergamum

ASIA

LYCIA

Myra

PHRYGIA

GALATIA

BITHYNIA
AND PONTUS

PAMPHYLIA

Alexandria

EGYPT

Memphis

Cyprus

CILICIA

CAPPADOCIA

COMMAGENE

JUDEA

Jerusalem

Sidon

SYRIA

Antioch

0
100
200
300 Kilometers

0
100
200
300 Miles

Jesus's Birth and Early Childhood

MEDITERRANEAN SEA

EGYPT

Alexandria

Pelusium

Wilderness
Of Shur

Joseph and his family flee to Egypt
because an angel forewarned them of
Herod's intent to murder Jesus.

Mary and Joseph return to
Palestine under divine guidance.

Jesus visits temple in
Jerusalem at the age of 12.

Gabriel announces to Mary
that she will bear a son.

Raphia

Gaza

Joppa

IDUMEA

Jerusalem

JUDEA

SAMARIA

Nazareth

GALILEE

Cana

Capernaum
Bethsaida

Bethlehem

Jordan R.

Birth of Jesus
(7-6 BC)

Jesus is brought to
Jerusalem for
sacrificial ceremony.

0
25
50
75
100 Kilometers

0
25
50
75
100 Miles

Luke Timeline

50–5 BC

MARCH 15, 44 BC
Augustus Caesar's reign begins.

39 BC
Roman Senate declares Herod king of the Jews.

37 BC
Herod assumes possession of the domain to which he had been named earlier.

20 BC
Herod begins thorough expansion of the temple in Jerusalem.

6 TO 4 BC
Imperial census in territory governed by Herod

5 BC–AD 9

6–4 BC
Jesus's birth

MARCH 12/13, 4 BC
Eclipse of the moon just before Herod's death

APRIL 11, 4 BC
Passover celebrated just after Herod's death

4 BC
Herod's sons, Herod Philip, Herod Antipas, and Archelaus, divide Palestine and rule three territories under the aegis of Rome.

AD 9
Jesus travels with his parents from Nazareth to Jerusalem for the Passover Festival.

AD 10–30

18–36
Caiaphas serves as high priest.

26–36
Pontius Pilate is prefect of Judea.

29
John the Baptist's ministry begins.

29
Jesus's baptism

29
Jesus's wilderness temptations

29
Jesus's call of his first disciples

30
The first Passover of Jesus's ministry, an occasion on which it was said that the temple (inner sanctuary) had stood for 46 years

30
Jesus goes from Judea to Galilee when he learns of John the Baptist's death.

AD 31–33

31
Second Passover of Jesus's ministry; he comes under increasing scrutiny for plucking grain on the Sabbath.

32
Jesus feeds the 5,000 around the time of his third Passover.

32–33
Between the Passover of 32 and 33, Jesus withdraws from public ministry and focuses on preparing his disciples. During this time period is Peter's confession at Caesarea Philippi and Jesus's transfiguration.

NISAN 14–16 OR APRIL 3–4, 33
Jesus's trials, death, and resurrection

Angelic Announcements in Luke

PASSAGE	ANGEL	RECIPIENT(S)	SUMMARY	RESPONSE
LUKE 1:5–25	Gabriel	Zechariah	The angel informed Zechariah that he and his wife, Elizabeth, would have a child in their old age.	Zechariah was overcome with fear, doubt, and questioning. "'How can I know this?' Zechariah asked the angel. 'For I am an old man, and my wife is well along in years'" (v. 18). As a result of his faithless response, Zechariah became mute until after the birth of his son, John the Baptist.
LUKE 1:26–38	Gabriel	Mary	The angel told the Virgin Mary that she would give birth to a son who would be "the Son of God" (v. 35).	"'I am the Lord's servant,' said Mary. 'May it happen to me as you have said.' Then the angel left her" (v. 38).
LUKE 2:8–20	An angel of the Lord	The shepherds	A proclamation that the Savior of the world was born	"Let's go straight to Bethlehem and see what has happened, which the Lord has made known to us" (v. 15).
LUKE 24:5–7	Two men in dazzling clothes	Women at the tomb	Proclamation of Jesus's resurrection and call to remember Jesus's promises about his resurrection	Remembered Jesus's promises, found the Eleven, and told them what they discovered (vv. 8–9)

The Work of the Spirit

OLD TESTAMENT	JESUS CHRIST	NEW TESTAMENT
God's Spirit hovered over the waters to carry out God's Word (Gen 1:2–3; Ps 33:6)	The Holy Spirit overshadowed Mary so that the Child she miraculously conceived would be called the Son of God (Luke 1:30–35)	The Holy Spirit dwells in believers as the firstfruits of the coming new creation (Rom 8:22–25)
The Spirit of the Lord anointed people for leadership over and service to God's people (Exod 35:30–35; 1 Sam 16:13)	God's Spirit descended upon Jesus at his baptism in the form of a dove, anointing him as God's Son and empowering his ministry as the Messiah (Matt 3:16–17; Luke 4:14–21)	The Holy Spirit testifies to God's children and gives gifts to them so they can lead and serve the body of Christ (Rom 8:14–17; 1 Cor 12)
The Lord led the Israelites in the wilderness for 40 years to humble them and test them (Deut 8:2)	The Spirit led Jesus into the wilderness to be tempted by the Devil after 40 days and nights of fasting (Matt 4:1)	The Holy Spirit leads Jesus's followers in carrying out the Great Commission (Matt 10:16–20; Acts 1:8)
The Spirit was promised to indwell God's people, to transform them and cause them to obey God's law (Ezek 36:25–27)	Jesus baptizes with the Holy Spirit, transforming his disciples (Matt 3:11)	The Spirit brings about the new birth so people can enter the kingdom of God (John 3:3–8,34; Titus 3:4–7)

John the Baptist's Life

OLD TESTAMENT PROPHECIES

FROM THE PROPHET ISAIAH

- A voice of one crying out (Isa 40:3–5; Matt 3:3)
  - *Prepare the way for the LORD in the wilderness*

FROM THE PROPHET MALACHI

- The Lord's messenger (Mal 3:1; Matt 11:10)
  - *Prepare the way before the LORD*
- Elijah the prophet (Mal 4:5; Matt 11:14; 17:11–13)
  - *Precedes the coming of the great and awesome Day of the LORD*

NEW TESTAMENT PROPHECIES

FROM THE ANGEL GABRIEL

- A son named John miraculously promised to childless Zechariah and Elizabeth in their old age (Luke 1:11–17)
  - *Will be filled with the Holy Spirit while in his mother's womb*
  - *Will go before the Lord in the spirit and power of Elijah*
  - *Will make ready for the Lord a prepared people*

IN THE WOMB

- Leaped in Elizabeth's womb at the hearing of Mary's greeting, who was pregnant with the Messiah (Luke 1:41–45)

IN THE WILDERNESS

- Grew up, became spiritually strong, and lived in the wilderness; wore a camel-hair garment and had a diet of locusts and wild honey (Luke 1:80; Matt 3:4)
- Preached in the wilderness (Matt 3:1–2)
  - *Repent, for the kingdom of heaven is at hand*
- Baptized people in the Jordan River as they confessed their sins (Matt 3:5–6)
- Confronted the Pharisees and Sadducees for their hypocrisy (Matt 3:7–10)
- Testified to the One coming after him who would baptize with the Holy Spirit (Matt 3:11–12)
- Baptized Jesus to fulfill all righteousness (Matt 3:13–17)
- Testified to the preexistent, supremely worthy Lamb of God, who takes away the sin of the world (John 1)

IN PRISON

- Arrested, chained, and put in prison because he told Herod it was unlawful to have his brother's wife as his own (Matt 4:12; 14:3–4)
- Sent word to Jesus by his disciples asking if he was the Messiah to come, experiencing some doubt as he languished in prison (Matt 11:2–6)
- Beheaded by Herod at the request of his wife and her daughter (Matt 14:6–11)
- Buried by his disciples (Matt 14:12)

HE MUST INCREASE, BUT I MUST DECREASE

Jesus described John the Baptist as the greatest of those born of women, though even the least in the kingdom is greater than him. John was sent by God to testify to the light, who is Jesus. He was a prophet of the Most High to prepare the way of the Lord, giving people knowledge of salvation through the forgiveness of sins. He baptized with water for repentance, but he steadfastly pointed to the One greater than him, the One who would baptize with the Holy Spirit. John was but a friend of the Groom, and he found great joy in Jesus's coming. With deep humility he preached about repentance and pointed people to the Lamb of God, who takes away the sin of the world.

Jesus's Exaltation

JESUS'S EXALTATION	OLD TESTAMENT TYPES AND PROPHECIES	RESPOND IN FAITH	RESPOND IN WORSHIP AND MISSION
The son of man was "lifted up" on a cross (John 12:32–33)	• Moses and all the prophets said the Messiah must suffer and enter into his glory (Luke 24:25–27)	• Everyone who believes in him will not perish but have eternal life (John 3:14–16)	• Preach Christ crucified, who is the power and wisdom of God (1 Cor 1:23–24)
The Messiah was raised from the dead (Matt 28:5–6)	• David prophesied that the Lord's Holy One would not experience decay (Ps 16:8–11; cp. Acts 2:24–32) • The Suffering Servant died for the sins of others and was vindicated with prolonged days (Isa 53:10–12)	• Blessed are those who believe in Jesus's resurrection, even without seeing him (John 20:27,29)	• Praise to "my Lord and my God" (John 20:28) • Call people to repentance because Jesus's resurrection proves that one day he will judge the world in righteousness (Acts 17:30–31)
The risen King was given all authority in heaven and on earth (Matt 28:18)	• One like a son of man given authority to rule over an everlasting, all-expansive kingdom (Dan 7:13–14)	• Confess with your mouth that Jesus is Lord and believe in your heart that God raised him from the dead and you will be saved (Rom 10:9)	• Go and make disciples of all nations, baptizing them in the name of the Father, Son, and Holy Spirit, and teaching them to observe everything Jesus commanded (Matt 28:19–20)
The risen King ascended into heaven with a cloud and sat down at the right hand of God, where he pours out the Holy Spirit on believers (Acts 1:9–11; 2:33–36)	• One like a son of man, with the clouds of heaven, went before the Ancient of Days and received authority to rule, glory, and a kingdom (Dan 7:13–14) • The Lord told David's Lord to sit at his right hand until his enemies are all conquered (Ps 110:1)	• Repent and be baptized in Jesus's name for the forgiveness of sins, and you will receive the promised Holy Spirit (Acts 2:38)	• Set your minds on things that are above, not on earthly things, because that is where Christ is seated (Col 3:1–17) • Use your gifts from Jesus through the Holy Spirit to serve others so God may be glorified through Jesus Christ in everything (1 Pet 4:10–11)
Jesus will come again on the final "day of the Lord," when every knee will bow and every tongue will confess that Jesus Christ is Lord as he vindicates his followers and conquers all his enemies (Phil 2:9–11; Rev 19–22)	• "God is my salvation" (Isa 12:1–6) • Every knee will bow and every tongue confess allegiance to the Lord as he puts his enemies to shame and justifies his people (Isa 45:21–25)	• Drawing near to God, believe that he exists and rewards those who seek him (Heb 11:6) • While doing what is good, entrust yourself to a faithful Creator and Savior (1 Pet 4:17–19)	• While looking forward to Christ's appearance, proclaim the gospel, endure hardship, do the work of an evangelist, and one day receive from the Lord the crown of righteousness (2 Tim 4:1–8)

The Messiah-King

THE DAVIDIC COVENANT	SOLOMON, SON OF DAVID	JESUS, *THE* SON OF DAVID
The Lord would make a house, a dynasty, for David and raise up his descendant to sit on his throne *(2 Sam 7:11–12)*	Solomon rode on David's mule to be anointed as king, and then he sat down on David's throne *(1 Kgs 1:32–40)*	Jesus is the promised Son of David, the Messiah-King who rode into Jerusalem on a donkey *(Matt 1:1–17; Luke 19:35; Zech 9:9)*
David's descendant would build a house, a temple, for the Lord's name *(2 Sam 7:13)*	Solomon built the temple for the Lord's name, and the glory of the Lord filled the temple *(1 Kgs 5–8)*	Jesus cleansed the temple in his zeal for the Lord's holiness, but even more so, he declared himself to be the temple of God, raised up in three days *(Luke 19:45–46; John 2:13–22)*
The Lord would be a father to David's descendant, and he would be a son to the Lord *(2 Sam 7:14)*	The Lord chose Solomon to be his son, and he would be his Father *(1 Chr 28:6)*	Jesus is the beloved Son of God *(Matt 3:16–17; 17:5; Luke 1:30–33; Heb 1:5)*
The Lord would discipline David's descendant but never remove his faithful love from him *(2 Sam 7:14–15)*	Solomon's many wives turned his heart away to follow other gods, so the Lord took away the peace of the kingdom and sent enemies against Solomon; he also took the kingdom away from Solomon's son, leaving only one tribe to him for the sake of David *(1 Kgs 11)*	Jesus is the Good Shepherd who laid down his life for his sheep, saving them from their sin so they will never lose God's faithful love *(Matt 26:26–29; John 10:11–18,27–30)*
David's house and kingdom will endure forever, and his throne will be established forever *(2 Sam 7:16)*	Solomon failed to persevere in keeping the Lord's commands, so his kingdom was not established forever *(1 Chr 28:7)*	Jesus has received all authority in heaven and on earth, and he will be with his disciples always, to the end of the age *(Matt 28:18–20; Luke 1:32–33)*

Christ as Priest

WHO WAS AN OLD TESTAMENT PRIEST?

REQUIREMENTS	DUTIES

• A Levite, a descendant of Levi
• Specifically, a descendant of Aaron
• Holy to the Lord
  – Physically without blemish
  – Ceremonially clean
  – Morally clean by virtue of prescribed sacrifices
	• Offer sacrifices to God on behalf of the people
	• Bless the people on behalf of God
	• Teach the people the law of God

THE LEVITES

Abraham

Levi

While Levi was known for his anger, fury, and cruelty in Genesis, his descendants the Levites sided with Moses for the holiness of God in the incident with the golden calf. They obeyed the Lord and were thus dedicated to the Lord for his service.

Gershon

Kohath

Merari

THE KOHATHITES were responsible for the most holy objects within the tabernacle.

Libni Shimei

Amram Izhar Hebron Uzziel

Mahli Mushi

THE GERSHONITES were responsible for the tabernacle's tent and coverings.

THE MERARITES were responsible for the tabernacle's supports.

Moses

Aaron

Nadab Abihu Eleazar Ithamar

Phinehas

NADAB AND ABIHU were killed by God for performing a priestly duty without following God's instructions.

THE DESCENDANTS OF AARON were responsible for sacrifices in the tabernacle and therefore rightly called priests.

WHO WAS AN OLD TESTAMENT HIGH PRIEST?

• A specific descendant of Aaron
• Appointed by God
• Had the responsibility of entering the most holy place once a year to make atonement for the people's sins on the Day of Atonement

WHO WERE SOME OF THE HIGH PRIESTS?

- AARON *(Exod 28:1; Heb 5:1–4)*
- ELEAZAR *(Num 20:25–28)*
- PHINEHAS *(Judg 20:27–28)*
- ELI *(1 Sam 1:9)*
- AHIMELECH *(1 Sam 21:1)*
- ABIATHAR *(1 Sam 23:9; Mark 2:26)*
- ZADOK *(1 Kgs 2:35)*
- JEHOIADA *(2 Kgs 12:2)*
- HILKIAH *(2 Kgs 22:8)*
- JOSHUA *(Hag 1:1; Zech 3:1)*
- ELIASHIB *(Neh 3:1)*

AARON

Aaron, along with his descendants after him, was appointed by God for the priestly ministry of offering sacrifices to God on behalf of the people and for blessing the people in the name of the Lord.

PHINEHAS

Phinehas was zealous among the Israelites with the Lord's zeal when he put a man and woman to death for blatant disobedience against God *(Num 25:1–13)*.

HOW WAS JESUS A PRIEST?

REQUIREMENTS	JESUS

• A Levite, a descendant of Levi
• Specifically, a descendant of Aaron
• Holy to the Lord
  – Physically without blemish
  – Ceremonially clean
  – Morally clean by virtue of prescribed sacrifices
	• The King, the Messiah, a descendant of the tribe of Judah (*Heb 7:14*)
	• Holy to the Lord (*Heb 4:15*)
	  – Tested in every way as we are, yet without sin
	• A priest in the order of Melchizedek, based not on physical genealogy but on the power of his indestructible life, having been raised from the dead never to die again (*Heb 7:15–17*)

HOW WAS MELCHIZEDEK THE GREAT HIGH PRIEST?

• Genesis 14:17–20; Psalm 110:4; Hebrews 7 • Name means "King of Righteousness" • King of Salem, or "King of Peace" • A priest of the Most High God • Blessed Abraham after a battle and received a tenth of Abraham's possessions	• Appears in Genesis (a book of beginnings, genealogies, births, and deaths) without father, mother, or genealogy, without a beginning of days or end of life • A king-priest who remains a priest forever, foreshadowing the Son of God (*Heb 7:3*)

HOW WAS JESUS THE GREAT HIGH PRIEST?

THE LEVITICAL HIGH PRIEST	JESUS THE GREAT HIGH PRIEST
Mediator of the old covenant (*Heb 9:1–10*)	Mediator of a new, better covenant (*Heb 9:11–28*)
Offered a sacrifice first for his own sin (*Heb 5:3*)	Tempted in every way as we are, yet without sin (*Heb 4:15*)
Appointed by God according to physical descent from Aaron (*Heb 5:4*)	Appointed by God not according to physical descent but in the order of Melchizedek (*Heb 5:5–6*)
Remained in the office of priest until death (*Heb 7:23*)	Remains a priest forever because he lives forever (*Heb 7:24*)
Offered sacrifices daily for the sins of the people and himself (*Heb 7:27*)	Offered himself once for all for the sins of the people (*Heb 7:27*)
Entered the most holy place only once a year with the blood of an animal to make atonement for himself and the people, but this sacrifice could never perfect the worshipper's conscience (*Heb 9:7,9*)	Entered the most holy place in heaven once for all with his own blood to make eternal atonement for the people and to cleanse their consciences from dead works to serve the living God (*Heb 9:14*)
Offered the same sacrifices year after year that could never perfect the worshipper (*Heb 10:1*)	Offered himself once for all to sanctify the worshipper (*Heb 10:10*)
Stood day after day offering the same ineffectual sacrifices (*Heb 10:11*)	Offered himself as the one effectual sacrifice for sins and sat down at the right hand of God (*Heb 10:12*)

The priests of the old covenant were appointed by God according to their lineage, being descendants of Aaron, the brother of Moses. These priests were to be holy and set apart to the Lord and, as Phinehas demonstrated, zealous for the Lord's holiness. The priesthood of Aaron served its purpose for a time but could never accomplish the ultimate goal of sanctification for the worshipper because of sin in both the priest and the people. Therefore, the kind of priest we need is one who is holy, innocent, undefiled, separated from sinners, and exalted above the heavens (*Heb 7:26*). Jesus is this high priest. This sinless Son of God is a priest forever in the order of Melchizedek (*Heb 7:17*). He is the unblemished Lamb of God (*John 1:29,36*) who offers himself once for all as the atoning sacrifice for the worshipper (*Heb 10:10*). He is zealous for his Father's holiness (*John 2:13–17*) and has sat down at the right hand of the Father in heaven, having completed his sacrificial work (*Heb 10:12*). As our Great High Priest, Jesus accomplishes the work of reconciling us to God. He is the One whose perfect righteousness is presented to the Father for our justification. He is the One who intercedes for us before the Father (*Heb 7:25; 9:24*) and prays for us to remain faithful (*Luke 22:31–32; John 17*). In him we find our forgiveness for sin and peace with God.

John

Genre | **GOSPEL, HISTORICAL NARRATIVE**

Jesus, the eternal Word and Son of God who became human,
reveals who God is through his teachings, miraculous
signs, death, and resurrection bringing life, light, and love
to the world, particularly to those who believe.

INTRODUCTION

AUTHOR   A close reading of the Gospel of John suggests that the author was an apostle (1:14; cp. 2:11; 19:35); one of the Twelve ("the one Jesus loved," 13:23; 19:26; 20:2; 21:20; cp. 21:24–25); and, still more specifically, John, the son of Zebedee (note the association of "the one Jesus loved" with Peter in 13:23–24; 18:15–16; 20:2–9; 21; and in Luke 22:8; Acts 1:13; 3–4; 8:14–25; Gal 2:9). The church fathers, too, attested to this identification (e.g., Irenaeus). Since the apostolic office was foundational in the history of the church (Acts 2:42; Eph 2:20), the apostolic authorship of John's Gospel invests it with special authority as firsthand eyewitness (John 15:27; 1 John 1:1–4).

BACKGROUND   The most plausible date of writing is the period between AD 70 (the date of the destruction of the temple) and 100 (the end of John's lifetime), with a date in the 80s most likely. A date after 70 is suggested by the references to the Sea of Tiberias in 6:1 and 21:1 (a name widely used for the Sea of Galilee only toward the end of the first century); Thomas's confession of Jesus as "my Lord and my God" in 20:28 (possibly a statement against emperor worship in the time of Domitian); the reference to Peter's martyrdom, which occurred in 65 or 66 (21:19); the lack of reference to the Sadducees, who ceased to be a Jewish religious party after 70; and the comparative ease with which John equated Jesus with God (1:1,14,18; 10:30; 20:28).

MESSAGE AND   The purpose statement in 20:30–31 indicates that John wrote with an evangelistic
PURPOSE   purpose, probably seeking to reach unbelievers through Christian readers of his Gospel. If the date of composition was after AD 70, the time of the destruction of the Jerusalem temple, it is likely that John sought to present Jesus as the new temple and center of worship for God's people in replacement of the old sanctuary.

SUMMARY   The Gospel of John is different from the Synoptic Gospels—Matthew, Mark, and Luke—in that more than 90 percent of its material is unique. John's Gospel does not focus on the miracles, parables, and public speeches that are so prominent in the other accounts. Instead, the Gospel of John emphasizes the identity of Jesus as the Son of God and how we, as believers, should respond to his teachings. John emphasized the deity of Jesus from the beginning of his Gospel. Eternal life is knowing God and Jesus Christ (17:3). Further, knowledge of God comes from believing and knowing Jesus. *Knowing* and *believing* are key terms for John.

STRUCTURE   John is divided into two main parts. In the first section (chaps. 2–11) the focus is on both Jesus's ministry to "the world" and the signs he performed. Jesus performs seven signs that meet with varying responses. The second major section (chaps. 12–21) reveals Jesus's teaching to his disciples and the triumphant "hour" of his passion.

Outline

I. **Prologue: Christ as the Eternal Word (1:1–18)**
   A. The Word (1:1)
   B. The Word and creation (1:2–5)
   C. The Word and the world (1:6–18)

II. **Presentation of Christ as the Son of God (1:19–12:50)**
   A. By John the Baptist (1:19–34)
   B. To his disciples (1:35–51)
   C. Through miraculous signs (2:1–12:50)

III. **Instruction of the Twelve by the Son of God (13:1–17:26)**
   A. The Last Supper (13:1–38)
   B. The way to the Father (14:1–31)
   C. The true vine (15:1–27)
   D. The gift of the Spirit (16:1–33)
   E. Jesus's high priestly prayer (17:1–26)

IV. **Suffering of Christ as the Son of God (18:1–20:31)**
   A. His arrest, trial, and death (18:1–19:42)
   B. His triumph over death (20:1–31)

V. **Epilogue: The Continuing Work of the Son of God (21:1–25)**
   A. Appearances to his disciples (21:1–14)
   B. Assignment to his disciples (21:15–25)

WORD STUDY

egō eimi

Greek pronunciation:
[eh GOH ay MEE]

CSB translation:
I am

Uses in John's Gospel: 76
Uses in the NT: 153

Focus passage:
John 18:5

The words *egō eimi* occur numerous times in the NT, but in John's Gospel they have a special meaning with two related connotations. First, *I am* often refers to Jesus's claim to be the Messiah. This is clear in John 4 where the woman at the well referred to the coming Messiah (v. 25) and Jesus responded, "I . . . am he [*egō eimi*]" (v. 26). This meaning of *egō eimi* also occurs in Jesus's words to the disciples, "*I am* telling you now before it [Judas's betrayal] happens, so that when it does happen you will believe that *I am* he [*egō eimi*]" (13:19). Jesus's foreknowledge of Judas's betrayal provided evidence for the other disciples that he was indeed the Messiah. Second, *egō eimi* often refers to Jesus's claim to deity. Instances like 8:58 probably reflect the burning bush episode when God revealed himself to Moses as "*I AM*" (Exod 3:14), as well as the use of *egō eimi* by God in the Greek of Isaiah (e.g., 41:4; 43:10; 48:12).

logos

Greek pronunciation:
[LAH gahss]

CSB translation:
word

Uses in John's Gospel: 40
Uses in the NT: 330

Focus passage:
John 1:1,14

Like the related verb *legō* (to speak), the noun *logos* most often refers to either oral or written communication. It means "statement" or "report" in some contexts, but most often in John's Gospel (and in the NT in general) *logos* refers to God's Word (that is, the OT) or to Jesus's words. Thus, the primary use of *logos* is to denote divine revelation in some form or another. John uses the term in its most exalted sense when he personifies *logos* to refer to Christ. The *Logos* eternally existed as God (the Son) and with God (the Father)—he was in fact the Creator (John 1:1–3)—but he became a human being (v. 14), Jesus of Nazareth, so that he could reveal the Father and his will for humanity (v. 18).

pisteuō

Greek pronunciation:
[pihss TYEW oh]

CSB translation:
believe

Uses in John's Gospel: 98
Uses in the NT: 241

Focus passage:
John 6:29–47

The Greek word *pisteuō* means "to believe, trust, rely upon," and its related noun is *pistis* (faith). In his Gospel, John never uses the words *repent, repentance,* or *faith* to describe the way people are saved. Instead, he used *believe* since this term included all these ideas. John preferred the verb form to emphasize the act that is necessary for someone to be saved—total dependence on the work of another. John does indicate, however, that *believing* can be superficial; that is, it can be merely intellectual without resulting in true salvation (2:23–24; 12:42–43; see Jas 2:19). But John's main point is that complete reliance upon Jesus, the Christ and Son of God (John 20:31), for salvation gives eternal life to the person who *believes* (3:16; 6:47). Jesus used a wordplay when he said that people must do "the work of God" for salvation, for his point was that we must not try to work for it at all. We must simply "*believe* in the one he has sent" (6:29).

John Timeline

AD 17–61

17
Ephesus experiences a destructive earthquake.

52
Paul travels through Ephesus toward the end of his second missionary journey.

52
Apollos comes to Ephesus and is mentored by Aquila and Priscilla.

54
Paul returns to Ephesus for a two-and-a-half-year ministry.

61
The Hittites destroy Babylon.

AD 62–67

62
Timothy, elder of Ephesus, receives first letter from Paul, 1 Timothy.

66
The Jewish War is started by Zealots, who drive the Romans out of Jerusalem temporarily.

67?
Timothy receives second letter from Paul, 2 Timothy.

AD 67–70s

64–67?
Deaths of Peter and Paul in Rome

66–70?
John leaves Jerusalem for Ephesus.

70
The Romans crush the Jewish rebellion and destroy Jerusalem and the temple.

70–100
John is spiritual leader of the church at Ephesus.

70s
John's Gospel written

73
Paul writes his letter to the Ephesians.

AD 80s–100

80s
John's letter (1 John) to the churches of Asia Minor

80s
John's letter to the elect lady (2 John)

80s
John's letter to Gaius (3 John)

95
John is exiled to Patmos and writes the book of Revelation.

100
Ephesus becomes one of the world's largest cities with a population approaching 500,000.

Eternal Life in John's Writings

REFERENCE	SCRIPTURE
JOHN 3:15	"… everyone who believes in him may have eternal life."
JOHN 5:24	"Truly I tell you, anyone who hears my word and believes him who sent me has eternal life and will not come under judgment but has passed from death to life."
JOHN 10:28	"I give them eternal life, and they will never perish. No one will snatch them out of my hand."
JOHN 17:3	"This is eternal life: that they may know you, the only true God, and the one you have sent—Jesus Christ."
1 JOHN 2:25	"And this is the promise that he himself made to us: eternal life."
1 JOHN 5:11	"And this is the testimony: God has given us eternal life, and this life is in his Son."
1 JOHN 5:20	"And we know that the Son of God has come and has given us understanding so that we may know the true one. We are in the true one—that is, in his Son, Jesus Christ. He is the true God and eternal life."

The Great "I AM"

I AM . . . (JOHN 8:58)	OLD TESTAMENT ALLUSION	THE METAPHOR'S EMPHASES	A DISCIPLE'S RESPONSE
The Bread of Life (*John 6:35,51*)	The Lord provided bread from heaven—manna—for the Israelites in the wilderness (*Exod 16*)	The Bread of Life from heaven—Jesus—satisfies and sustains for eternal life (*John 6:33,47,50–51,58*)	• Come to Jesus and believe in him (*John 6:35*) • Feast upon Jesus's flesh and blood (*John 6:51–58*)
The Light of the World (*John 8:12; 9:5*)	The Lord led the Israelites in the wilderness at night in a pillar of fire (*Exod 13:21–22*)	The Light of the World provides the light of life, which gives spiritual sight for direction and work (*John 8:12; 9:4,35–39*)	• Believe in Jesus, the Son of Man, and worship him (*John 9:35–38*) • Follow Jesus (*John 8:12*)
The Gate for the Sheep (*John 10:7,9*)	The Gate of the Lord through which the righteous enter his presence (*Ps 118:17–24*)	The Gate secures salvation, good pasture, and abundant life for the sheep (*John 10:9–10*)	• Listen to Jesus (*John 10:8*) • Enter by Jesus (*John 10:9*)
The Good Shepherd (*John 10:11,14*)	The Lord promised to shepherd his sheep himself through a human shepherd, "my servant David" (*Ezek 34:11–31*)	The Good Shepherd knows his sheep and lays his life down for the sheep to secure their eternal life (*John 10:11,15,17–18,28*)	• Listen to the voice of Jesus and follow him (*John 10:3–4,16,27*)
The Resurrection and the Life (*John 11:25*)	The Lord raises the dead and gives them new, fresh life (*Isa 26:19*)	The Resurrection and the Life has the power to raise the dead to eternal life, both physically and spiritually (*John 11:25–26*)	• Believe in Jesus and see the glory of God (*John 11:25,40*)
The Way, the Truth, and the Life (*John 14:6*)	The Lord teaches the way, reveals the truth, and rescues the believer's life from death (*Ps 86:11–13*)	The Way, the Truth, and the Life is preparing a place for his followers to enjoy eternal life in the presence of the Father and Jesus (*John 14:1–6*)	• Believe in God and believe in Jesus (*John 14:1*)
The True Vine (*John 15:1,5*)	The Lord promised that his vineyard would fill the whole world with fruit (*Isa 27:2–6*)	The True Vine provides life to the branches—Jesus's disciples—so they can be fruitful (*John 15:1–8*)	• Remain in Jesus and he and his words in you (*John 15:4–5,7*) • Keep Jesus's commands—namely, love one another (*John 15:9–17*)

Witnesses of Jesus's Resurrection

Mary Magdalene	**JOHN 20:11–18**
Mary Magdalene, Mary the mother of James, Salome, and Joanna	**MATTHEW 28:1; MARK 16:1; LUKE 24:10**
Cleopas and a comrade on the road to Emmaus	**LUKE 24:13–35**
Simon Peter	**LUKE 24:34; JOHN 1:42**
The disciples, minus Thomas	**LUKE 24:36–43; JOHN 20:19–25**
The disciples, including Thomas	**JOHN 20:26–28**
Seven disciples by the Sea of Tiberias: Simon Peter, Thomas, Nathanael from Cana of Galilee, Zebedee's sons, and two other disciples	**JOHN 21:1–23**
The eleven disciples and a crowd at a Galilean mountain	**MATTHEW 28:16–17**
James and then to all the apostles	**1 CORINTHIANS 15:7**
The disciples and the more than 500 brethren from the church in Jerusalem	**LUKE 24:49–53; ACTS 1:3–11**
Other convincing proofs	**ACTS 1:3**

Jesus's Signs

	MIRACLE	LOCATION	METHOD
FIRST SIGN	Turning Water into Wine (*John 2:1–12*)	Cana of Galilee	Jesus asked for six stone jars to be filled with water, and then the water became wine
SECOND SIGN	Healing an Official's Son (*John 4:46–54*)	Cana of Galilee/ Capernaum	Jesus, in Cana, told the official his son, in Capernaum, would live, and he recovered at that very hour
THIRD SIGN	Healing a Man Disabled for 38 Years (*John 5:1–18*)	Jerusalem, at the Pool of Bethesda	Jesus told the disabled man to get up, pick up his mat, and walk, which he did instantly
FOURTH SIGN	Feeding of 5,000 (*John 6:1–15; see also Matt 14:13–21; Mark 6:30–44; Luke 9:10–17*)	Near the Sea of Galilee	Jesus gave thanks for five barley loaves and two fish from a boy and distributed them to the people through the disciples
FIFTH SIGN	Walking on Water (*John 6:16–21; see also Matt 14:22–33; Mark 6:45–52*)	On the Sea of Galilee	Jesus walked on the water to the disciples in a boat in a storm
SIXTH SIGN	Healing a Man Born Blind (*John 9*)	Jerusalem	Jesus spit on the ground, made some mud, spread the mud on the man's eyes, and told him to wash in the pool of Siloam
SEVENTH SIGN	Raising Lazarus from the Dead (*John 11*)	Bethany, near Jerusalem	Jesus prayed and shouted, "Lazarus, come out!"

John's Gospel was written with a singular purpose—so that his readers would believe Jesus is the Messiah, the Son of God, and by believing have eternal life in his name (John 20:30–31). While making references to many signs that Jesus performed, John highlighted seven specific signs through the first part of his Gospel to support this purpose.

	WITNESSES	PURPOSE	RESULT
FIRST SIGN	Jesus's disciples and the servants at the wedding	Revealed Jesus's glory as the Son of God (*John 2:11*)	Jesus's disciples believed in him (*John 2:11*)
SECOND SIGN	The royal official and his whole household	—	The royal official and his household believed in Jesus (*John 4:53*)
THIRD SIGN	The man who was healed, and later some of the Jews who objected to him carrying his mat on the Sabbath	Demonstrated Jesus's unity with the Father and authority over the Sabbath (*John 5:17–18*)	The Jews began persecuting Jesus because he healed and encouraged "work" on the Sabbath and made himself equal to God (*John 5:16,18*)
FOURTH SIGN	The disciples and the crowd of 5,000 men	Demonstrated Jesus was greater than Moses, and he is the bread of life (*John 6:32–35*)	The crowd believed Jesus was the Prophet and wanted to make him king by force, but he withdrew from them (*John 6:15*)
FIFTH SIGN	The disciples	Demonstrated Jesus's identity as "I AM" (*Exod 3:14; John 6:20*)	—
SIXTH SIGN	The disciples, the formerly blind man, his parents, his neighbors and those who had seen him begging, and the Pharisees	Displayed God's works in the man's healing (*John 9:3*)	The man believed in Jesus and worshipped him (*John 9:38*)
SEVENTH SIGN	Mary, Martha, the Jews who had come to comfort them, the disciples, and Lazarus	Displayed God's glory and glorified the Son of God (*John 11:4*)	Many believed in Jesus, but the Sanhedrin plotted to kill him (*John 11:45–53*)

Who Was at the Cross?

WITNESSES AT THE CROSS	MATTHEW (CHAPTER 27)	MARK (CHAPTER 15)	LUKE (CHAPTER 23)	JOHN (CHAPTER 19)
Roman soldiers	X	X	X	X
Simon of Cyrene	X	X	X	
Two criminals	X	X	X	X
The centurion	X	X	X	
Jewish officials (chief priests, scribes, and elders)	X	X	X	X
Passersby who mocked Jesus	X	X		
Many other women (daughters of Jerusalem)	X	X	X	X
Mary Magdalene	X	X	X	X
Mary (mother of James and Joseph/Joses)	X	X		X
Salome	X	X	X	X
Mary, Jesus's mother	X	X		
The unnamed disciple				X
Joseph of Arimathea**	X	X	X	X
Nicodemus**				X

**Received permission to take away Jesus's body.

John's Gospel was written that "whoever believes" might receive the gift of "life" in Jesus' name (3:16; 17:2–3; 20:31). According to the Fourth Gospel, that gift of life is characterized by a personal knowledge of God the Father, through God the Son (17:3), a knowledge enabled by God the indwelling Holy Spirit (15:26; 16:13–15). Eternal life thus consists in more than simply the removal of sin or an escape from death, though to be sure, both belong to John's teaching about salvation. Eternal life has a positive, trinitarian character. . . . Eternal life thus consists in sharing in the gracious overflow of the Father's eternal love for the Son in the Spirit. We share in this gracious overflow as "children" (1:12) who have been grafted into God's beloved Son as branches into the true vine (15:1–11; 17:26).

○

ANDREAS J. KÖSTENBERGER AND SCOTT R. SWAIN[2]

Timeline of Jesus's Last Week

Barren Fig Tree Cursed
Matthew 21:18–19

Temple Cleansed of Money Changers
Matthew 21:12–13; Mark 11:12–19

Greeks Seek Jesus
John 12:20–26

Anointing of Jesus at Bethany
Matthew 26:6–13;
Mark 14:3–9;
John 12:3–8

Sunday   Monday   Tuesday   Wednesday

Triumphal Entry
Matthew 21:1–10;
Mark 11:1–10

At the Temple Complex
Matthew 21:14–16;
Mark 11:11a

Return to Bethany
Matthew 21:17;
Mark 11:11b

Debates at the Temple
Matthew 21:23–23:39;
Mark 11:27–12:40

End-Time Discourse at the Mount of Olives
Matthew 24:1–25:46;
Mark 13

Jesus's Trials in Jerusalem
Matthew 26:57–68; 27:1–2,11–26

Jesus's Resurrection
and Appearances
Matthew 28:1–10,16–20;
John 20–21

Jesus's Crucifixion, Death, and Burial
Matthew 27:27–61; John 19:16–42

Thursday Friday Saturday Sunday

Passover Celebrated;
Lord's Supper Inaugurated
Matthew 26:17–30

Jesus in the Tomb
Matthew 27:62–66;
Luke 23:55b

Jesus's Farewell Discourses
John 14–16

Jesus's Intercessory Prayer
John 17

Prayer of Agony in Gethsemane
Matthew 26:36–46; Mark 14:32–42

Jesus's Betrayal and Arrest
Matthew 26:47–56; Mark 14:43–50

Acts

Genre | **HISTORICAL NARRATIVE**

Following his ascent to heaven, Jesus continued his work to bring about the kingdom of God by sending the Holy Spirit to empower the apostolic community to proclaim the gospel message and establish the church throughout the ends of the earth.

INTRODUCTION

AUTHOR

The book of Acts is formally anonymous. The traditional view is that the author was the same person who wrote the Gospel of Luke—Luke the physician and traveling companion of Paul (Col 4:14; 2 Tim 4:11; Phlm 24). As early as the second century AD, church leaders such as Irenaeus wrote that Luke was the author of Acts. Irenaeus and many scholars since his time have interpreted the "we" passages to mean that the author of Acts was one of the eyewitness companions of Paul (see Acts 16:10–17; 20:5–15; 21:1–18; 27:1–29; 28:1–16). Luke fits this description better than any other candidate, especially given the similar themes between the Gospel of Luke and the book of Acts.

BACKGROUND

The date of composition of the book of Acts is to a large extent directly tied to the issue of authorship. A number of scholars have argued that Acts should be dated to the early 60s (at the time of Paul's imprisonment). Acts closes with Paul still in prison in Rome (28:30–31). Although it is possible that Luke wrote at a later date, a time when Paul had been released, it is more plausible to think that he completed this book while Paul was still in prison. Otherwise he would have ended the book by telling about Paul's release.

MESSAGE AND PURPOSE

The book of Acts emphasizes the work of God through the Holy Spirit in the lives of people who devoted themselves to Jesus Christ, especially Paul as he led the Gentile missionary endeavor. It is no exaggeration to say that the Christian church was built through the dynamic power of the Spirit working through chosen vessels. Another important concept is the radial spread of the gospel from Jews to Gentiles, from Jerusalem to Judea, from Samaria and on to the rest of the world (1:8). Thus Christianity transformed from being a sect within Judaism to a world religion that eventually gained acceptance everywhere, even in the heart of the pagan Roman Empire: Rome itself.

SUMMARY

The book of Acts provides a glimpse into the first three decades of the early church (ca. AD 30–63) as it spread and multiplied after the ascension of Jesus Christ. It is not a detailed or comprehensive history. Rather, it focuses on the role played by apostles such as Peter, who ministered primarily to Jews, and Paul, the apostle to the Gentiles.

STRUCTURE

So far as literary form is concerned, the book of Acts is an ancient biography that focuses on several central characters, especially Peter and Paul. Acts 1:8 provides the introduction and outline for the book. Once empowered by the Holy Spirit, the disciples proclaimed the gospel boldly in Jerusalem. As the book progresses, the gospel spread further into Judea and Samaria, and then finally into the outer reaches of the known world through the missionary work of Paul.

Outline

I. **Empowerment for the Church (1:1–2:47)**
   A. Waiting for power (1:1–26)
   B. The source of power (2:1–13)
   C. Pentecostal witness to the dispersion (2:14–47)

II. **Early Days of the Church (3:1–12:25)**
   A. In Jerusalem (3:1–7:60)
   B. In Samaria: the Samaritan Pentecost (8:1–25)
   C. To the ends of the earth: Philip's witness (8:26–40)
   D. Conversion and preparation of Paul (9:1–31)
   E. In Judea: Peter in Caesarea (9:32–11:18)
   F. To the ends of the earth (11:19–12:25)

III. **Paul's First Missionary Journey (13:1–14:28)**
   A. Cyprus (13:1–12)
   B. Pisidian Antioch (13:13–52)
   C. Iconium (14:1–7)
   D. Lystra, Derbe; return to Antioch (14:8–28)

IV. **The Jerusalem Council (15:1–35)**

V. **Paul's Second Missionary Journey (15:36–18:22)**
   A. Antioch to Troas (15:36–16:10)
   B. Troas to Athens (16:11–17:34)
   C. Corinth (18:1–22)

VI. **Paul's Third Missionary Journey (18:23–21:16)**
   A. The Ephesian Pentecost (18:23–19:41)
   B. Macedonia to Troas, Athens, Corinth, and return (20:1–21:16)

VII. **Paul En Route to and in Rome (21:17–28:31)**
   A. In Jerusalem (21:17–23:35)
   B. In Caesarea (24:1–26:32)
   C. Voyage to Rome (27:1–28:15)
   D. Ministry at Rome (28:16–31)

onoma

Greek pronunciation:
[AH nah mah]

CSB translation:
name

Uses in Acts: 60
Uses in the NT: 231

Focus passage:
Acts 3:6,16

The Greek noun *onoma* means "name" and has several uses, such as the following: (1) It is used for proper names of persons and places. (2) In Revelation 3:1 *onoma* is rendered "reputation," as in the expression *he has made a name for*. (3) It also occurs in the sense of *title*, as in Matthew 10:41 (the literal *in the name of a prophet* means "because he is a prophet" or "because he has the title *prophet*"). In Hebrews 1:4 *onoma* refers to "Son" as the name or title that is more excellent than the angels' (see vv. 2,5,8), and in Philippians 2:9 the "name that is above every name" is the title "Lord" (*kurios*), as explained in v. 11. (4) Finally, the NT often demands that believers act for, or in the name of, Jesus Christ. The phrase "in Jesus's name" is not a mystical formula attached to the end of a prayer. It's an expression of faith that identifies the person whom believers serve (Matt 18:20; Acts 2:38).

ekklēsia

Greek pronunciation:
[ehk lay SEE ah]

CSB translation:
church

Uses in Acts: 23
Uses in the NT: 114

Focus passage:
Acts 5:11

The Greek noun *ekklēsia* refers to a people gathered together—that is, an assembly or congregation. In secular Greek, *ekklēsia* was commonly used for the assembled citizens of a city (see Acts 19:32,39–40).

In the NT, *ekklēsia* is found in the Gospels only three times, all in Matthew (16:18; 18:17). It occurs in Acts more than any other book, and 62 times in Paul's letters. Jesus stated that he would build the *ekklēsia* (Matt 16:18) and that the *ekklēsia* must exercise discipline on members who sin (Matt 18:15–17). In the former passage Jesus used *ekklēsia* in a corporate sense (all believers), and in the latter passage in the local sense (believers in a specific assembly).

Christianos

Greek pronunciation:
[krihss tee ah NAHSS]

CSB Translation:
Christian

Uses in Acts: 2
Uses in the NT: 3

Focus passage:
Acts 11:26

From the Greek noun *Christos* (*Christ* or *Messiah*) comes the word **Christianos**, meaning "belonging to Christ." The term occurs in only three places in the NT. Acts 11:26 explains that it was in Antioch that the disciples were "first called *Christians*." The famine mentioned in the following verses occurred in AD 46 and indicates the term's usage entered sacred vocabulary about that time. Since this new word for followers of Christ was coined in Antioch rather than Israel, it may indicate that the *Christian* movement was being recognized among Gentiles as something distinct from Judaism and not just another Jewish sect. In Acts 26:28, Agrippa referred to Paul's attempt to persuade the king to become a *Christian*—an attempt Paul admitted applied not only to Agrippa but to everyone who was listening to his words of testimony (v. 29). Peter uses the term in reference to suffering "as a *Christian*" (1 Pet 4:16).

Acts Timeline

AD 33–37

NISAN 14–16 OR APRIL 3–5, 33
Jesus's trials, death, resurrection, and ascension

33
Pentecost

OCTOBER 34
Saul's conversion on the Damascus road

34–37
Paul's years in Arabia

37?
Paul's first visit to Jerusalem following his conversion

AD 37–41

SUMMER 37–40
Paul returns to his native Tarsus.

37–41
Caligula, emperor of Rome

SUMMER 40
Barnabas travels from Antioch of Syria to find Paul.

40
Conversion of Cornelius and his family

41
Barnabas and Saul serve together in Antioch.

AD 41–49

41–54
Claudius, emperor of Rome

44–47
Believers respond to famine prophesied by Agabus.

44
Martyrdom of James, son of Zebedee

44
Death of Herod Agrippa

47–49
Paul, Barnabas, and John Mark make their first missionary journey.

AD 49–62

49–52
Paul and Silas take their second missionary journey.

53–57
Paul's third missionary journey

57–59
Paul's arrest in Jerusalem and imprisonment in Caesarea

LATE 59
Paul's journey to Rome

60–62
Paul's house arrest in Rome

Pentecost and
the Jewish Diaspora

BLACK SEA

Sinope

Rome
Pompeii
Thessalonica
Philippi
(Istanbul)
PONTUS

ADRIATIC SEA
AEGEAN SEA
ASIA
CAPPADOCIA
Tigris R.
Nisibis

Ephesus
Antioch
MESOPOTAMIA

Corinth
PHRYGIA
Athens
PAMPHYLIA
Tarsus
Euphrates R.

Antioch
(Syria)

MEDITERRANEAN SEA
Myra
Paphos

Damascus

Babylon
Susa

Cyrene
Jerusalem

CYRENAICA

LIBYA
EGYPT
ARABIA

Alexandria

PERSIAN GULF

Heracleopolis

0   100   200   300   400 Miles

0   100 200 300 400 Kilometers

Nile R.

Thebes

RED SEA

Elephantine

Miracles in the Early Church (Acts 1–12)

MIRACLE	ACTS 1–12
The day of Pentecost	ACTS 2:2–11
The apostles perform many wonders and signs	ACTS 2:43
A lame man is healed	ACTS 3:7–11
An earthquake at a prayer meeting occurs	ACTS 4:31
Ananias and Sapphira drop dead	ACTS 5:1–10
An angel rescues the apostles from jail	ACTS 5:17–25
Stephen performs wonders and signs	ACTS 6:8
Many possessed, paralyzed, or lame are healed	ACTS 8:6–13
Samaritans receive the Holy Spirit	ACTS 8:14–17
Philip is carried away by the Spirit of the Lord	ACTS 8:39
Paul's Damascus road conversion occurs	ACTS 9:1–9
Saul's blindness is cured	ACTS 9:17–18
The paralytic Aeneas is healed	ACTS 9:32–35
Dorcas is restored to life	ACTS 9:36–42
An angel rescues Peter from prison	ACTS 12:6–17
Herod dies	ACTS 12:21–23

Early Church Leaders (Acts 1–12)

PETER

Peter is credited with being a leader of the twelve disciples. He frequently served as the spokesman for the disciples and was usually the one who raised the questions they all seemed to be asking. Jesus often singled out Peter for teachings intended for the entire group of disciples. Peter was committed to serving as a bridge in the early church, doing more than any other to hold together the diverse strands of primitive Christianity.

MATTHIAS

Matthias became a witness of Jesus's resurrection and took Judas's place as one of the twelve disciples.

JOHN

The apostle John appears three times in the book of Acts, and each time he is with Peter (1:13; 3:1–11; 4:13,20; 8:14). After Peter healed a man, they were arrested, imprisoned, and then released. They were "uneducated and untrained men" (4:13), but they answered their accusers boldly: "For we are unable to stop speaking about what we have seen and heard" (4:20). Later, John and Peter were sent to Samaria to confirm the conversion of Samaritans (8:14).

STEPHEN

The first Christian martyr, Stephen was foremost of those chosen to bring peace to the quarreling church (Acts 6:1–7) and so mighty in the Scriptures that his Jewish opponents in debate could not refute him as he argued that Jesus was the Messiah (6:10). Saul of Tarsus heard Stephen's speech to the Jewish Sanhedrin accusing the Jewish leaders of rejecting God's way as their forefathers had (6:12–7:53). Saul held the clothes of those who stoned Stephen to death; he saw him die a victorious death. Stephen may well have been the human agency that God used to conquer him who would become the greatest Christian missionary: Paul.

DORCAS

Dorcas was a Christian woman of Joppa who was known for her charitable works (Acts 9:36). She was also called Tabitha, an Aramaic name. When she became sick and died, friends sent for the apostle Peter. He came to Joppa. Through him Dorcas was restored to life. This was the first such miracle performed through any of the apostles, and it resulted in many new believers.

PHILIP

A member of the Jerusalem church, Philip was chosen as one of the first deacons (Acts 6:5). Following Stephen's martyrdom, he took the gospel to Samaria, where his ministry was blessed (8:5–13). He introduced the Ethiopian eunuch to Christ and baptized him (8:26–38). Philip was then transported by the Spirit to Azotus (Ashdod), where he conducted an itinerant ministry until taking up residence in Caesarea (8:39–40). Then, for nearly 20 years, we lose sight of him. He is last seen in Scripture when Paul lodged in his home on his last journey to Jerusalem (21:8).

BARNABAS

Barnabas sold his property and gave the proceeds to the Jerusalem church (Acts 4:36–37). The church chose Barnabas to go to Syrian Antioch to investigate the unrestricted preaching to the Gentiles there. He became the leader to the work and secured Saul (Paul) as his assistant. On Paul's first missionary journey, Barnabas at first seems to have been the leader (chaps. 13–14). Paul and Barnabas were sent to Jerusalem to try to settle the questions of how Gentiles could be saved and how Jewish Christians could have fellowship with them (15:1–21).

ANANIAS

Ananias was a disciple who lived in the city of Damascus (Acts 9:10–19). In response to a vision he received from the Lord, Ananias visited Saul (Paul) three days after Saul had his Damascus road experience. Ananias laid his hands on Saul, after which Saul received both the Holy Spirit and his sight. Acts 9:18 may imply that Ananias was the one who baptized Saul.

CORNELIUS

Cornelius was a centurion in the Roman army (Acts 10:1). Although he was a Gentile, he was a worshipper of the one true God who treated the Jewish people with kindness and generosity. After an angel appeared to him, he sent to Joppa for Simon Peter, who came to him with the message of forgiveness of sins through faith in Christ. Cornelius became a Christian as a result of this incident, marking the beginning of the church's missionary activity among Gentiles. It also helped raise the question of the possibility of salvation for those who were not Jews.

JAMES

As one of the twelve disciples (Acts 1:13), James, with Peter and John, formed Jesus's innermost circle of associates. These three were present when Jesus raised Jairus's daughter, witnessed the transfiguration, and were summoned by Christ for support during his agony in Gethsemane. James's zeal was revealed in a more selfish manner as he and John sought special positions of honor for the time of Christ's glory (Mark 10:35–40). They were promised, however, only a share in his suffering. Indeed, James was the first of the Twelve to be martyred (Acts 12:2).

Discourses in Acts

Peter's Mission Sermons

SCRIPTURE	LOCATION/AUDIENCE	THEME
Acts 2:14–41	An international group of God-fearing Jews in Jerusalem for Pentecost	The gift of the Holy Spirit proves now is the age of salvation. Jesus's resurrection validates his role as the Messiah.
Acts 3:11–26	A Jewish crowd in the Jerusalem temple	The healing power of Jesus's name proves that he is alive and at work. Those who rejected the Messiah in ignorance can still repent.
Acts 4:8–12	Jerusalem	There is salvation in no one else but Jesus Christ.
Acts 5:29–32	The Sanhedrin, Israel	We must obey God rather than men.
Acts 10:27–48	The Gentile Cornelius and his household, Caesarea	God accepts persons of all races who respond in faith to the gospel message.

Stephen's Sermon

SCRIPTURE	LOCATION/AUDIENCE	THEME
Acts 7	The Sanhedrin	God revealed himself outside the Holy Land. God's people capped a history of rejecting the leaders he had sent them by killing the Messiah.

Paul's Mission Sermons

SCRIPTURE	LOCATION/AUDIENCE	THEME
Acts 13	Jews in the synagogue in Pisidian Antioch	Paul's mission sermons illustrate the changing focuses of early Christian mission work: first Jewish evangelism, second Gentile evangelism, third development of Christian leaders.
Acts 17	Pagan Greeks at the Areopagus in Athens	
Acts 20	From Miletus to the elders of the Ephesian church	

Paul's Defense Sermons

SCRIPTURE	LOCATION/AUDIENCE	THEME
Acts 22:1–21	Jews in the synagogue in Pisidian Antioch	Paul's defense sermons stressed that he was innocent of any breach of Roman law. Paul was on trial for his conviction that Jesus had been raised from the dead and had commissioned Paul as a missionary to the Gentiles.
Acts 24:10–21	The Roman governor Felix	
Acts 26	The Jewish king Agrippa II	

The Jerusalem Council

HOLINESS CODE *LEVITICUS 17–18*	JERUSALEM COUNCIL *ACTS 15:19–21, 28–29*
Anyone from the house of Israel or from the aliens who reside among them . . .	*Because of the Jews in every city, Gentile believers . . .*
• Do not make pagan sacrifices *(17:3–9)*	• Should abstain from things polluted by idols
• Do not have illicit sexual relations of any kind *(18:6–23)*	• Should abstain from sexual immorality
• Do not eat animals without draining the blood [e.g., strangulation] *(17:13–14)*	• Should abstain from eating anything that has been strangled
• Do not eat blood *(17:10–12)*	• Should abstain from blood
Preserved the distinction of the Israelite people by prohibiting the detestable pagan practices of the Egyptians and the Canaanites *(18:1–5, 24–30)*	Preserved the distinction and unity of the church by facilitating the fellowship between Jewish and Gentile believers *(15:21–33)*

Paul's Missionary Journeys

Legend:
- City
- PAUL'S FIRST MISSIONARY JOURNEY
- PAUL'S SECOND MISSIONARY JOURNEY
- PAUL'S THIRD MISSIONARY JOURNEY
- PAUL'S VOYAGE TO ROME

Paul spends two years preaching the gospel as he awaits his appeal to Nero.

Ship lost in storm

Paul speaks to the Areopagus.

Luke joins Paul.

Paul restores life to young Eutychus.

Proconsul Sergius Paulus converted

Porcius Festus sends Paul to Rome to appeal to Caesar.

Jerusalem Council AD 49

Paul and Barnabas mistaken for gods.

Paul resumes his missionary travels.

Seas and regions:
- MEDITERRANEAN SEA
- ADRIATIC SEA
- AEGEAN SEA
- BLACK SEA
- CYRENAICA
- EGYPT
- ITALIA
- SICILY
- MALTA
- CRETE
- CYPRUS
- MACEDONIA
- THRACE
- ASIA
- BITHYNIA AND PONTUS
- GALATIA
- CAPPADOCIA
- LYCIA
- PHRYGIA
- PAMPHYLIA
- CILICIA
- COMMAGENE
- SYRIA
- DEAD SEA

Cities:
- Rome
- Puteoli
- Syracuse
- Rhegium
- Delphi
- Corinth
- Thessalonica
- Amphipolis
- Berea
- Neapolis
- Philippi
- Pergamum
- Ephesus
- Laodicea
- Colossae
- Lystra
- Derbe
- Perga
- Attalia
- Antioch
- Tarsus
- Damascus
- Jerusalem
- Sidon
- Tyre

Scale: 0 — 150 — 300 Kilometers / 0 — 150 — 300 Miles

83

The Promise of Acts

The book of Acts begins with two significant and related promises: first, Jesus said the Holy Spirit would come to empower his disciples; second, this power would enable them to be Jesus's witnesses in the city of Jerusalem, in the regions of Judea and Samaria, and to the ends of the earth (Acts 1:4–8). The rest of the book of Acts tells of the fulfillment of these promises.

JERUSALEM

Obeying the last instructions of Jesus, the disciples returned to Jerusalem and waited there for the Father's gift. After 10 days of praying together, the Holy Spirit filled the disciples, who spoke in different tongues. In this way, Peter and the apostles preached the gospel in Jerusalem to Jews from every nation—3,000 believed and were baptized (2:1–41).

Peter healed a lame man and preached the gospel to the gathering crowd—many believed, and the number of men came to 5,000. Peter and John were arrested and threatened, but filled with the Holy Spirit, Peter spoke boldly and defied the Sanhedrin's threats, choosing to obey God rather than men (3:1–4:22; cp. 5:12–42).

Stephen, one of seven men full of the Holy Spirit and chosen to care for the daily ministry of the church, performed signs, withstood detractors to the faith, and responded to the Sanhedrin with truth and conviction, such that he was stoned to death, the first Christian witness to die for his testimony to Jesus (6:1–7:60).

> After Stephen's death, "severe persecution broke out against the church in Jerusalem, and all except the apostles were scattered throughout the land of Judea and Samaria. . . . Those who were scattered went on their way preaching the word" (8:1,4).

JUDEA AND SAMARIA

Philip, one of the seven, went to a city in Samaria and proclaimed the Messiah to them and performed signs, and the believers were baptized. Peter and John prayed for the Samaritan believers and laid hands on them, and they received the Holy Spirit. Later, Philip was sent by an angel to the desert road to Gaza to share the good news about Jesus with an Ethiopian eunuch, and he baptized the Ethiopian (8:5–40).

Saul set off for Damascus to arrest believers, but Jesus appeared to him on the road, and Saul became his instrument to take his name to Gentiles, to kings, and to the Israelites—a mission he began to obey immediately. So the church throughout Judea, Galilee, and Samaria had peace and was strengthened. Because believers lived in the fear of the Lord and were encouraged by the Holy Spirit, the church increased in numbers (9:1–31).

The Lord brought Cornelius, a Gentile God-fearer, and Peter together so that Peter could bear witness to the good news of Jesus and Cornelius could become a believer in Jesus Christ. Cornelius and all the Gentiles who were with him to hear Peter's message received the Holy Spirit, speaking in other tongues and declaring the greatness of God; then they were baptized (10:1–48).

> The severe persecution after Stephen's death scattered people even beyond Judea and Samaria, as far as Phoenicia, Cyprus, and Antioch (11:19).

TO THE ENDS OF THE EARTH

Some believers from Cyprus and Cyrene arrived in Antioch and began to speak the gospel to the Greeks, and a large number believed. Barnabas was sent to Antioch; being full of the Holy Spirit, he encouraged them in the faith, and large numbers were added to the Lord (11:19–24).

Barnabas searched out Saul in Tarsus and brought him to Antioch to help teach. Later, the Holy Spirit told the leaders of the church at Antioch to set apart Barnabas and Saul for a specific mission, so they fasted, prayed, laid hands on them, and sent them off (11:25–26; 13:1–3).

Hearing the Old Testament in the New

GOD ALONE To Whom Every Knee Will Bow and Every Tongue Swear Allegiance (*Isa 45:22–23*)	**JESUS** Every Knee Will Bow and Every Tongue Will Confess Jesus Is Lord (*Phil 2:9–11*)
THE TOWER OF BABYLON God Confused Humanity with Different Languages (*Gen 11:1–9*)	**PENTECOST** The Filling with the Holy Spirit Overcame Language Barriers (*Acts 2:1–13*)
THE PROMISE OF THE SPIRIT God Will Pour Out His Spirit on All Humanity (*Joel 2:28–32*)	**THE OUTPOURING OF THE SPIRIT** The Promise of the Spirit Fulfilled (*Acts 2:14–21*)
OPPOSITION TO THE MESSIAH The Nations Plot in Vain against the Lord's Anointed (*Ps 2*)	**OPPOSITION TO THE CHURCH** The Messiah's People Prayed for Boldness (*Acts 4:23–31*)
A PROPHET LIKE MOSES God Promised to Raise Up a Prophet of His Word (*Deut 18:15–19*)	**JESUS** The Prophet God Raised Up to Turn People from Their Evil Ways (*Acts 3:19–26*)
ACHAN AND HIS FAMILY Stoned to Death for Disobedience to God's Word (*Josh 7*)	**ANANIAS AND SAPPHIRA** Dropped Dead for Lying to the Holy Spirit (*Acts 5:1–11*)
THE SUFFERING SERVANT Like a Lamb Led to the Slaughter for His People (*Isa 53:7–8*)	**JESUS** The Good News of the Sacrificial Lamb of God for Our Sin (*Acts 8:26–35*)
THE LORD Called Prophets for His Name to His People and the Nations (*Jer 1; Ezek 2*)	**JESUS** Called Saul to Take His Name to Gentiles, Kings, and Israelites (*Acts 9; 22; 26*)
THE LORD'S SERVANT A Light for the Nations; Salvation to the Ends of the Earth (*Isa 49:6*)	**PAUL AND BARNABAS** An Extension of the Work of Jesus, the Lord's Servant (*Acts 13:47*)
DAVID'S HOUSE The Nations That Bear God's Name Will Be Included (*Amos 9:11–12*)	**THE CHURCH** The Gentiles Who Are Called by Jesus's Name Are Included (*Acts 15:14–19*)
ADAM The First Man God Created, from Whom All Humanity Descends (*Gen 1–2*)	**PAUL'S CONNECTION** Idolaters Owe Their Worship to the One True God (*Acts 17:24–29*)

Spirit-Led Giving

ACTS OF GIVING	THE RESULTS	CHARACTERISTICS OF SPIRIT-LED GIVING
The believers held everything in common, so they sold possessions and property and distributed the proceeds to those among them in need (*Acts 2:44–45; 4:32*)	An international group of God-fearing Jews in Jerusalem for Pentecost	In love, Jesus laid down his life for us, so we should lay down our lives for our brothers and sisters in Christ and take care of their needs (*1 John 3:16–17*)
Peter and John did not have silver or gold to give but gave to a lame man what they did have and healed him in the name of Jesus Christ (*Acts 3:1–7*)	The lame man jumped up and entered the temple—walking, leaping, and praising God—giving Peter an opportunity to preach Christ to the gathering crowd (*Acts 3:8–26*)	Whatever you do, in word or in deed, do everything in the name of the Lord Jesus, giving thanks to God the Father through him (*Col 3:17*)
Joseph, also called Barnabas, sold a field he owned and brought the money and laid it at the apostles' feet (*Acts 4:36–37*)	Barnabas set an example of Spirit-led giving for the early church and all readers of the book of Acts	Each person should do as he has decided in his heart, not out of reluctance or necessity, for God loves a cheerful giver (*2 Cor 9:7*)
Ananias and Sapphira sold a piece of property and laid the proceeds at the apostles' feet as if it were all of it, but secretly they kept back part of the money for themselves (*Acts 5:1–2*)	They lied to God in testing the Holy Spirit and dropped dead for their deceit; great fear came on the whole church and on all who heard about these things (*Acts 5:3–11*)	We must love not in word or speech only but in action and truth (*1 John 3:18*)
Simon the Samaritan saw Peter and John lay hands on the Samaritan believers and them receive the Holy Spirit, so he offered money in order to obtain this power for himself (*Acts 8:18–19*)	Peter rebuked Simon, saying one cannot obtain the gift of God with money; he commanded Simon to repent of his wickedness and to pray to the Lord for forgiveness (*Acts 8:20–24*)	Salvation and the Holy Spirit are gifts from God that cannot be bought and sold—freely you have received; freely give (*Matt 10:8; 1 Cor 2:12*)
A prophesied famine throughout the Roman world prompted the Jewish and Gentile Christians in Antioch to send relief to the brothers and sisters in Judea, each giving according to his ability (*Acts 11:27–29*)	Barnabas and Saul (Paul) were sent from Antioch with the gift to the elders of the Jerusalem church, highlighting the unity of the church across geographical and ethnic lines (*Acts 11:30*)	Our giving should testify to our faith in Christ so that God will be glorified and the church will be unified (*2 Cor 9:12–14*)
After Lydia and the Philippian jailer each believed in the Lord, they welcomed Paul and Silas into their homes to care and provide for them (*Acts 16:13–15,25–34*)	Lydia's house appears to have become a meeting place for the church in Philippi (*Acts 16:40*)	Share with the saints in their needs and pursue hospitality (*Rom 12:13*)
Paul was a tentmaker by trade, which provided for his own needs and the needs of his missionary partners and prevented him from becoming a burden to others as he shared the gospel (*Acts 18:1–4; 20:33–34*)	Paul demonstrated the necessity of helping the weak by the work of your hands and illustrated the truth of Jesus's words "It is more blessed to give than to receive" (*Acts 20:35*)	Work with your own hands so you are not dependent upon anyone and have something to share with those in need; in this way you will be a godly example in the presence of unbelievers (*Eph 4:28; 1 Thess 4:11–12*)

Suffering for Jesus

ACTS OF MINISTRY	THE RESPONSE OF ENEMIES	THE FORM OF PERSECUTION	THE RESULTS
Peter, along with John, healed a lame man and then preached in Jesus's name to the gathering crowd (Acts 3:1–26)	The Jewish leaders were annoyed because Peter and John taught the people and proclaimed in Jesus the resurrection of the dead (Acts 4:1–2)	Peter and John were arrested by the Sanhedrin and threatened if they spoke in Jesus's name again (Acts 4:3–22)	They reported the events to the church and then all prayed to the Lord for boldness in the face of opposition, which the Lord granted through his Holy Spirit (Acts 4:23–31)
Through the apostles, the sick and those with unclean spirits were being healed (Acts 5:12–16)	The high priest and the Sadducees were filled with jealousy (Acts 5:17)	The apostles were arrested and tried by the Sanhedrin, flogged, and ordered not to speak in Jesus's name (Acts 5:18–41)	The apostles rejoiced that they were counted worthy to suffer for Jesus's name and continued proclaiming the good news about Jesus (Acts 5:41–42)
Stephen performed great wonders and signs among the people and spoke with wisdom from the Holy Spirit (Acts 6:8–10; 7:1–53)	Some Jews from the Freedmen's Synagogue opposed Stephen and argued with him (Acts 6:9)	• Stephen was falsely accused of blasphemy against the temple (Acts 6:11–14; cp. Matt 26:59–61) • He was taken outside the city and stoned to death (Acts 7:57–60; cp. Luke 23:32–33)	• Stephen prayed for Jesus to receive his spirit (Acts 7:59; cp. Luke 23:46) • He prayed for forgiveness for those stoning him (Acts 7:60; cp. Luke 23:34) • Persecution broke out against the church and scattered believers throughout the world; they preached the word about Jesus (Acts 8:1,4; 11:19–20)
Saul's persecution of the church was persecution of Jesus Christ, the head of the church; Jesus called Saul to himself as his chosen instrument to take his name to Gentiles, to kings, and to the Israelites, and Saul would now suffer for the name of Jesus (Acts 9:1–19)			
—	—	Herod violently attacked some of the church; he executed James, John's brother, with the sword and arrested Peter to try and execute him (Acts 12:1–5)	Peter rescued from prison by an angel (Acts 12:6–19)
Paul and Barnabas preached the gospel to both Jews and Gentiles in Pisidian Antioch (Acts 13:13–44)	The Jews were filled with jealousy at the gospel preached to Gentiles and rejected it (Acts 13:45–47)	The Jews stirred up persecution against Paul and Barnabas and had them expelled from the district (Acts 13:50)	Paul and Barnabas shook the dust off their feet against the Jews and moved on to preach elsewhere; the disciples left behind were filled with joy and the Holy Spirit (Acts 13:51–52)
Paul, along with Barnabas, healed a lame man and preached the gospel in Lystra (Acts 14:8–10)	Some Jews from Pisidian Antioch and Iconium came and won over the crowds against Paul and Barnabas (Acts 14:19)	Paul was stoned and dragged out of the city; people thought he was dead (Acts 14:19)	Paul miraculously recovered and went back into the city, and the next day left for Derbe (Acts 14:20)
Paul, along with Silas, freed a slave girl from demonic possession in the name of Jesus (Acts 16:16–18)	The slave girl's owners realized their hope for profit from her predictions of the future was gone (Acts 16:19)	Paul and Silas were arrested, severely flogged, and imprisoned with their feet in the stocks (Acts 16:19–24)	They prayed and sang hymns to God in prison before an earthquake freed them; then they shared the gospel with the jailer, who believed along with his entire household (Acts 16:25–34)

Paul strengthened the disciples on his first missionary journey by telling them, "It is necessary to go through many hardships to enter the kingdom of God" (Acts 14:22). In this he echoed Jesus's words to his disciples: "You will have suffering in this world. Be courageous! I have conquered the world" (John 16:33).

Paul's Life

THE PHARISEE

- A Jew born in Tarsus but trained in Jerusalem by Gamaliel; zealous for God (Acts 22:3)
- Agreed with the stoning of Stephen and persecuted the church; traveled to Damascus to arrest believers and bring them back to Jerusalem (7:58; 8:1,3; 9:1–2; 22:4–5)

THE CHRISTIAN

- Met Jesus on the way to Damascus and was blinded; three days later, he was healed by Ananias so he could see, be filled with the Holy Spirit, and be baptized (9:3–18)
  - *Jesus's chosen instrument to take his name to Gentiles, kings, and Israelites, and he would suffer for Jesus's name (9:15)*
- Proclaimed Jesus in the synagogues in Damascus and later in Jerusalem (9:20–30)
  - *The Jews conspired to kill him; he escaped to Jerusalem and then to Tarsus*
- Found by Barnabas in Tarsus and taken to Antioch to help teach the disciples (11:25–26)

THE MISSIONARY

- Saul and Barnabas set apart by the Spirit for missionary calling (13:1–3)

THE LETTERS OF PAUL

FIRST MISSIONARY JOURNEY (ACTS 13:4–14:28)

GALATIANS

Proclaimed the word of God in the synagogues throughout Cyprus. In Pisidian Antioch, Jews rejected the word while Gentiles received it; subsequently expelled from the district. Some in Iconium attempted to stone them. In Lystra, they were mistaken for the Greek gods Zeus and Hermes; later, Jews stirred up the crowd and they stoned Paul, but he miraculously recovered. Preached in Derbe and then revisited some of the previous cities, warning of hardship and establishing church leadership; then sailed back to Antioch and reported about their trip and the faith of the Gentiles.

- Sent with Barnabas to the Jerusalem Council, which discussed and affirmed salvation by faith for Gentiles (15:1–35)

SECOND MISSIONARY JOURNEY (ACTS 15:36–18:22)

1 THESSALONIANS
2 THESSALONIANS

Parted ways with Barnabas over a disagreement regarding John Mark, so Paul took Silas and went through Derbe, Lystra, and Iconium, strengthening the churches and taking along Timothy. Forbidden by the Spirit to minister in Asia and Bithynia; received a vision while in Troas and headed to Macedonia to preach the gospel. Ministry in Philippi led to being flogged and imprisoned. A mob and riot in Thessalonica forced them to flee; they experienced a similar situation in Berea. Preached the gospel in Athens. Met Aquila and Priscilla in Corinth and stayed there for a year and a half speaking about Jesus. Briefly shared the gospel in Ephesus. Then visited Jerusalem and returned to Antioch.

THIRD MISSIONARY JOURNEY (ACTS 18:23–21:19)

1 CORINTHIANS
2 CORINTHIANS
ROMANS

Traveled through Galatia and Phrygia strengthening the disciples. Ministered in Ephesus for three years, evangelizing throughout all of Asia. After a riot, Paul traveled to Macedonia and then went to Greece. A Jewish plot forced him back through Macedonia and then to Troas. Eventually Paul came to Miletus, where he met with the elders from Ephesus before journeying on to Jerusalem.

- Seized in the Jerusalem temple by a mob and taken out to be killed, but rescued by the Roman regiment; a plot against him caused him to be moved to Caesarea, where he made a defense before Felix and later Festus before appealing to Caesar after two years in custody; he also made a defense before King Agrippa (21:26–26:32)

EPHESIANS
PHILIPPIANS
COLOSSIANS
PHILEMON

Sent to Rome by ship for trial before Caesar; shipwrecked at Malta for three months; finally arrived at Rome, where he was placed under house arrest for two years, and yet, he still proclaimed the kingdom of God and taught about Jesus with boldness and without hindrance with all those who visited him (27:1–28:31)

1 TIMOTHY
2 TIMOTHY
TITUS

According to tradition, released from house arrest by Caesar and continued his missionary ministry; arrested a second time and imprisoned in Rome, where he was beheaded, according to tradition

- *Paul fought the good fight, finished the race, and kept the faith (2 Tim 4:7)*

Paul's Persecutions

SAUL AS THE PERSECUTOR

As an ideal Pharisee Paul was probably active as a Jewish missionary winning Gentiles as proselytes. He may have been like the Pharisees Jesus described who traveled "over land and sea to make one convert" (Matt 23:15). Paul, more than his mentor, Gamaliel (Acts 5:34–39), recognized the serious threat that the followers of Jesus posed to the traditional Jewish religion. The Mishnah taught that a Jewish male was ready for a position of authority at age 30. Thus Paul was probably in his thirties when he, with authorization from the chief priest, began to imprison believers first in the synagogues of Jerusalem and then later in Damascus.[3] His persecution of believers continued:

- At the stoning of Stephen (Acts 7:57–60)
- Ravaging the church (Acts 8:1–4)
- Taking believers as prisoners (Acts 9:1–2)
- Pursued and punished Christians (Acts 26:9–11)
- Intensely persecuted the church (Gal 1:13)

SAUL'S TURNING POINT

Around AD 35, while Saul was on his way to Damascus to arrest and imprison believers there, the resurrected and glorified Christ appeared to him with blinding radiance. After encountering Jesus on the Damascus road, Saul began proclaiming Jesus as the Messiah (Acts 9:19b–22; 1 Tim 1:12–15).

PAUL AS THE RECIPIENT OF CHRISTIAN PERSECUTION

While Paul was in the temple performing a ritual to demonstrate his Jewish faithfulness to some of the Jerusalem believers, Jewish opponents incited a riot, and he was arrested (AD 57). Paul was sent to Caesarea to stand trial before the procurator Felix (Acts 23). After two years of procrastination on the part of his detainers, Paul finally appealed to the Roman emperor for trial. After arriving in Rome, Paul spent two years under house arrest awaiting his trial. Paul wrote Philemon, Colossians, Ephesians, and Philippians during this first Roman imprisonment.[4] Throughout Paul's missionary journeys he encountered many types of persecution:

- Threatened (Acts 9:23,29)
- Expelled (Acts 13:50)
- Mistreated and stoned (Acts 14:5–19)
- Stripped, beaten with rods, flogged, and jailed in stocks (Acts 16:22–24)
- Mobbed (Acts 17:5–14)
- Mocked (Acts 17:18)
- Attacked (Acts 18:12)
- Plotted against (Acts 20:3)
- Seized, dragged out, almost murdered, bound, and mobbed (Acts 21:30–36)
- Sent before the Sanhedrin (Acts 23:1–8,10)
- Imprisoned and accused (Acts 27–28)

THE PERSECUTION OF ALL CHRISTIANS

According to church tradition, Paul was arrested again and subjected to a harsher imprisonment. He was condemned by the emperor Nero and beheaded with the sword at the third milestone on the Ostian Way, at a place called Aquae Salviae. He is buried on the site covered by the Basilica of St. Paul Outside the Walls. Paul's execution probably occurred in AD 67.[5]

ACTS

Expansion of the Early Church

SEA OF
GALILEE

Nazareth

Peter meets
with Cornelius.

Caesarea Maritima

Philip preaches
throughout Samaria.

Philip settles in
Caesarea Maritima.

Peter raises
Tabitha (Dorcas)
to life.

Peter and John are
sent to investigate
claims that Samaritans
are receiving the gospel
preached by Philip.

Peter heals
Aeneas, a paralytic.

Joppa

Lydda

Gophna

Philip preaches
in Azotus.

Peter and
John are
arrested.

Jericho

Azotus
(Ashdod)

Jerusalem

Bethlehem

Stephen is
stoned to death.

MEDITERRANEAN SEA

DEAD
SEA

Gaza

Philip baptizes an
Ethiopian official
and explains the
words of Isaiah.

| 0 | 10 | 20 Miles |
| 0 | 10 | 20 Kilometers |

- City
- PHILIP'S TRAVELS
- PETER AND JOHN'S TRAVELS
- PETER'S TRAVELS

The People of God

OLD TESTAMENT PROPHECY	NEW TESTAMENT CONNECTION
God promised Abraham (the father of many nations), Isaac, and Jacob that all the peoples of the world would be blessed through them and their offspring (*Gen 12:1–3; 17:3–8; 22:15–18; 26:2–5; 28:10–15*)	Those who have faith in Jesus, from both the Jews and the Gentiles, are considered Abraham's sons and blessed with him and through his offspring, who is Jesus (*Gal 3:7–9,16*)
The Lord chose Israel out of all the peoples on the earth to love, yet he shows no partiality and loves the resident alien (*Deut 10:14–19*)	Peter recognized that God shows no favoritism and accepts from every nation people who fear him and do what is right, believing in Jesus (*Acts 10:34–48*)
God is sovereign over all the nations, and his salvation is available to them; all the ends of the earth will fear him (*Ps 67*)	Jesus sent his witnesses to the ends of the earth (*Acts 1:8*), where every nation has been sovereignly placed so they might seek after God and find Jesus (*Acts 17:26–31*)
All the nations are commanded to praise the Lord because his faithful love to the world is great and his faithfulness endures forever (*Ps 117*)	Paul commanded the Gentile believers in Rome to glorify God for his mercy because they had been incorporated into the people of God by faith in Jesus (*Rom 15:7–13*)
Paul and Barnabas preached the gospel to both Jews and Gentiles in Pisidian Antioch (*Acts 13:13–44*)	Simeon recognized the baby Jesus as a light to the Gentiles (*Luke 2:28–32*), and Paul and Barnabas understood their mission to the Gentiles as fulfilling the Servant's purpose (*Acts 13:46–49*)
The Suffering Servant will be a light to the nations, taking salvation to the ends of the earth (*Isa 42:6; 49:6*)	The Holy Spirit came upon the Gentiles who believed (*Acts 10:44–48*) since there is no distinction between Jews and Gentiles who call upon the name of the Lord (*Rom 10:11–13*)
God promised that he would pour out his Spirit on all humanity and that everyone who calls on the name of the Lord will be saved (*Joel 2:28–32*)	The apostle James recognized that repentance and faith in Jesus among the Gentiles fulfilled the promise of the Messiah's ministry to save both Jews and Gentiles (*Acts 15:13–18*)

Romans

Genre | **EPISTLE**

The gospel of God, which is the announcement that the crucified and risen Jesus is the Messiah promised in Israel's Scriptures from long ago, brings justification and new life to Jews and Gentiles alike by faith alone and therefore serves as the basis for equality, unity, and fellowship within the church.

INTRODUCTION

AUTHOR   Paul the apostle is the stated and indisputable author of the book of Romans. From the book of Acts and statements in Romans, we learn that Paul wrote this letter while he was in Corinth and on his way to Jerusalem in the spring of AD 57 to deliver an offering from the Gentile churches to poor Jewish Christians (Acts 20:3; Rom 15:25–29).

BACKGROUND   All of Paul's writings grew out of his missionary/pastoral work and were about the problems and needs of local churches. The book of Romans is also of this genre, but it is the least "local" in the sense that Paul had not yet been to Rome. This letter was his opportunity to expound the good news message (the gospel). He could discuss the essence of sin, the salvation accomplished on the cross, the union of the believer with Christ, how the Spirit works in the Christian to promote holiness, the place of the Jewish people in God's plan, future things, and Christian living or ethics. Though Paul did not write Romans as a systematic theology, his somewhat orderly exposition has been the fountain for the development of that discipline.

MESSAGE AND PURPOSE   Paul's purpose in writing Romans can be identified from his direct statements in the text and inferred from the content. He expressly wrote that he wanted to impart spiritual strength to the believers at Rome (1:11–12; 16:25–26). The content of the letter shows that the churches experienced tensions between believers from different backgrounds. Paul wanted them to be united and to avoid dissension and false teaching (16:17–18). The content also reveals his exposition of what is essential Christianity and what are matters of indifference.

SUMMARY   Paul's letter to the Roman house churches has been preeminent among the New Testament writings for its theological and pastoral influence. It focuses on the doctrine of salvation, including the practical implications for believers as they live out the salvation given to them through Jesus Christ.

STRUCTURE   Paul wrote 13 of the 21 Letters (or "Epistles") contained in the New Testament. The four Gospels, the book of Acts, and the book of Revelation are not classified as letters. Romans is the longest of Paul's letters, and it contains the elements found in a standard letter at that time: a salutation (1:1–7), thanksgiving (1:8–17), the main body (1:18–16:18), and a farewell (16:19–24). Some scholars refer to Romans as a tractate (a formal treatise). But it bears all the marks of a real letter, although it is a fine-tuned literary composition.

Outline

hilastērion

Greek pronunciation:
[hih lahss TAY ree ahn]

CSB translation:
mercy seat

Uses in Romans: 1
Uses in the NT: 2

Focus passage:
Romans 3:25

The Greek noun *hilastērion* in Romans 3:25 is rich with theological meaning. The only other place this term occurs in the NT is Hebrews 9:5, which says that the cherubim above the ark of the covenant in the most holy place were "overshadowing the mercy seat." In the Greek OT, the word is used for the lid of the ark of the covenant (see Exod 25:17–22; Lev 16:2,13–15). Another related word, *hilasmos, atoning sacrifice*, occurs twice in the NT (1 John 2:2; 4:10). This word family refers to the turning away of God's wrath against sin by means of a sacrifice. The main ideas of this word group are *mercy* and *satisfactory sacrifice for sin*. The innermost part of the tabernacle was the place where mercy was found, but only through the proper sacrifice. Similarly, Jesus's death is the only place one can find mercy. God's wrath against sin was turned away by Christ's sacrifice.

charis

Greek pronunciation:
[KAH rihss]

CSB translation:
grace

Uses in Romans: 24
Uses in the NT: 155

Focus passage:
Romans 5:2

The Greek noun *charis* refers to an unmerited favorable disposition toward someone or something. In the NT, *charis* is commonly used in relation to salvation, especially in Paul's writings. Paul used *charis* to explain that salvation comes from God's own choice to show favor in redeeming lost persons through faith in Christ (see Rom 5:1–2; Eph 2:8–9; 2 Tim 1:9). However, God's undeserved favor is not toward those who have done nothing offensive; rather, God shows *grace* toward those who have sinned against him and are actually his enemies.

In Romans 5, Paul explained that peace with God is an act of God's *grace* (vv. 1–2). He reminded believers that at one time they were God's enemies (v. 10; see Eph 2:1–16; Col 1:21–22). Therefore, a better NT definition of *charis* would be *unmerited favor toward an enemy* or *grace* toward one who has forfeited any claim on God's favor because of sin and who deserves the opposite—God's judgment (Rom 5:9).

hamartia

Greek pronunciation:
[hah mahr TEE ah]

CSB translation:
sin

Uses in Romans: 48
Uses in the NT: 173

Focus passage:
Romans 14:23

The Greek noun *hamartia* is the most common term in the NT for human violation of God's moral standard. The related verb *hamartanō* (43 uses in the NT, 17 in Paul's letters) means *to fail* and *to do wrong*. *Hamartanō* came to include the idea *to sin*, which is the meaning of the verb in the NT. Both *hamartanō* and *hamartia* occur quite frequently in the Greek OT, mainly to translate the most common Hebrew words for sin.

In Romans 14 Paul said, "Everything that is not from faith is *sin*" (v. 23). The essence of *sin* is unbelief, so every violation of God's standard is a lack of faith in him. God doesn't want superficial obedience to a standard; he wants us to trust him completely (see Heb 11:6).

Romans Timeline

800–450 BC

753
Mythical founding of Rome by Romulus and Remus

753–509
Rome ruled by seven kings

509
King Tarquin the Proud ousted and the Roman Republic founded

494
Plebeian struggle with patricians results in greater voice in the governance of Rome.

460–438
Lucius Quinctius Cincinnatus, farmer, general, and consul of Rome

450–250 BC

451
A *Decemviri*, committee of 10 men, is commissioned to draw up Rome's first code of law, *The Twelve Tables*, binding on both patricians and plebeians.

312
The Via Appia, first of an unparalleled system of roads in the ancient world, is begun by Appius Claudius Caecus and runs in a southwesterly direction out of Rome.

275–272
Rome gains control of the entire Italian peninsula as a prelude to far greater expansion and a series of wars with other people.

269
The Romans begin minting coins.

264
The first recorded gladiatorial games in Rome during the funeral of Junius Brutus. Three pairs of gladiators fight to the death.

100 BC–AD 33

85 BC
Romans develop the hypocaust, a central heating system, used in large villas and public baths.

MARCH 15, 44 BC
Julius Caesar is assassinated.

27 BC–AD 14
Octavian (Augustus), the first emperor of the Roman Empire

5 BC
The birth of Jesus of Nazareth

AD 14–37
The reign of Tiberius Caesar

AD 33–80

33
Jesus's trials, crucifixion, resurrection, and ascension

OCTOBER 34
Saul's conversion on the Damascus road

49
Agrippina, Emperor Claudius's third wife, brings Seneca out of an eight-year exile on Corsica to be the tutor of her son Nero.

54
Agrippina poisons her husband, Claudius; her son Nero becomes the last Roman emperor of the Julio-Claudian dynasty.

57
Paul's letter to the church at Rome written in Corinth

64
Nero blames Christians for the great fire in Rome.

70–80
Roman Colosseum under construction

Key Words in Romans

ATONEMENT: In his atoning work, Christ is both representative and substitute in our place. Reconciliation between God and humanity was affected by the death, burial, and resurrection of Jesus Christ.

FAITH: Trusting commitment of one person to another, particularly of a person to God. Faith is the central concept of Christianity. One may be called a Christian only if one has faith.

FLESH: Biblically, the flesh is viewed as the created and natural humanity. It is not automatically sinful, but it is weak, limited, and temporal. Such qualities make it vulnerable to sin. Since sin promises pleasure and fulfillment, the natural propensity is for the flesh to yield to sin's promises.

GLORY: The weighty importance and shining majesty that accompany God's presence. The basic meaning of the Hebrew word *kabod* is "heavy in weight." To give glory is to praise or recognize the importance of another, especially God.

GOSPEL: The English word used to translate the Greek word for "good news." Christians use the word to designate the message and story of God's saving activity through the life, ministry, death, and resurrection of God's unique Son, Jesus.

GRACE: Undeserved acceptance and love received from another, especially the characteristic attitude of God in providing salvation for sinners.

JUSTIFICATION: The process by which an individual is brought into an unmerited, right relationship with another, whether that relationship is established between people or with God.

LAW: The law of God as contained in the Old Testament. "Law of sin" referred to the conduct that's determined by sin. "Law of faith" referred to conduct determined by faith in God.

PROMISE: God's pronouncement of his plan of salvation and blessing to his people, one of the unifying themes integrating the message and the deeds of the Old and New Testaments.

RIGHTEOUSNESS: In biblical usage, righteousness is rooted in covenants and relationships. Righteousness is the fulfillment of the terms of a covenant between God and humanity or between humans in the full range of human relationships.

SALVATION: The acutely dynamic act of snatching others by force from serious peril. In its most basic sense, salvation is the saving of a life from death or harm. Scripture, particularly in the New Testament, extends salvation to include deliverance from the penalty and power of sin.

SANCTIFICATION: The process of being made holy, resulting in a changed lifestyle for the believer. Sanctification is vitally linked to the salvation experience and is concerned with the moral and spiritual obligations assumed in that experience. We were set apart for God in conversion, and we are living out that dedication to God in holiness.

SIN: Actions by which humans rebel against God, miss his purpose for their lives, and surrender to the power of evil rather than to God.

WORKS: Deeds leading to planned results, both by God and people. God's works are his acts and deeds in creating, saving, and sustaining. Jesus Christ came to do the work of God, testifying to his divine nature and mission. Christ calls and enables his followers to continue his works.

New Testament Letters

MEDITERRANEAN SEA

ARIATIC SEA

AEGEAN SEA

BLACK SEA

Rome

Syracuse

Rhegium

Larissa

Corinth

Cenchreae

Athens

Phoenix

CAUDA

Fair Havens

Lasea

CRETE

Salmone

Ephesus

Philippi

Neapolis

Lystra

Derbe

Tarsus

Antioch

Caesarea Maritima

Antipatris

JUDEA

Jerusalem

Paul wrote to Rome before being imprisoned and executed there.

Paul and Apollos ministered in Corinth at different times (Acts 18:1–19:1).

Paul planted the church at Philippi on his second missionary journey.

Paul left Titus in Crete to help establish the church there.

Paul wrote to Timothy while he was pastoring in Ephesus.

Peter wrote to Christians scattered throughout these provinces (1 Pet 1:1).

Paul wrote to the Galatian churches planted during his first missionary journey.

Paul confronted Peter for hypocrisy against the Gentiles.

James, the brother of Jesus, was the leader of the Jerusalem church.

0
100
200
300 Miles

0
100
200
300 Kilometers

Doctrinal Emphases in Paul's Letters

PAUL'S LETTERS	PURPOSE	MAJOR DOCTRINE(S)	KEY PASSAGE
Romans	To express the nature of the gospel, its relation to the Old Testament and Jewish law, and its transforming power	Salvation	Romans 3:21–26
1 Corinthians	To respond to questions about marriage, idol food, and public worship; to discourage factions; to instruct on resurrection	The Church, the Resurrection	1 Corinthians 12:12–31; 15:1–11
2 Corinthians	To prepare readers for Paul's third visit and to defend Paul and the gospel he taught against false teachers	The Church, Jesus Christ, Salvation	2 Corinthians 5:11–6:2
Galatians	To stress freedom in Christ against Jewish legalism while avoiding moral license	Salvation	Galatians 2:15–21
Ephesians	To explain God's eternal purpose, grace, and the goals God has for the church	Salvation, the Church	Ephesians 2:1–22
Philippians	To commend Epaphroditus; to affirm generosity; to encourage unity, humility, and faithfulness even to death	Christian Unity, Joy in Salvation	Philippians 1:3–11
Colossians	To oppose false teachings related to a matter and spirit dualism and to stress the complete adequacy of Christ	Jesus Christ	Colossians 1:15–23
1 Thessalonians	To encourage new converts during persecution, to instruct them in Christian living, and to assure them concerning the second coming	Last Things	1 Thessalonians 4:13–18
2 Thessalonians	To encourage new converts in persecution and to correct misunderstandings about the Lord's return	Last Things	2 Thessalonians 1:3–12
1 Timothy	To encourage Timothy as minister, to refute false doctrine, and to instruct about church organization and leadership	Church Leaders	1 Timothy 3:1–15
2 Timothy	To encourage Christians in the face of persecution and false doctrine	Education	2 Timothy 2:14–19
Titus	To instruct church leaders, to advise about groups in the church, and to teach Christian ethics	Salvation	Titus 2:11–14
Philemon	To effect reconciliation between a runaway slave and his Christian master	Christian Ethics	Philemon 8–16

Paul's Letters

	LETTER	PURPOSE
PAUL'S FIRST MISSIONARY JOURNEY AD 47–49	Galatians	Paul wrote to defend his authority as an apostle and to teach that sinners are justified and live godly lives by trusting in Jesus.
PAUL'S SECOND MISSIONARY JOURNEY AD 49–52	1 Thessalonians	Paul addressed questions from the church and encouraged their faith.
	2 Thessalonians	Paul clarified how to live the Christian life in light of Christ's return.
PAUL'S THIRD MISSIONARY JOURNEY AD 54–56	1 Corinthians	Paul emphasized the necessity of accepting the Lord's authority.
	2 Corinthians	Paul defended his authority and ministry as commissioned by Christ and empowered by the Spirit.
	Romans	Paul outlined practical implications for believers as they live out their salvation through Jesus Christ.
PAUL'S FIRST ROMAN IMPRISONMENT AD 60–62	Ephesians	Paul emphasized the grace of God toward sinners in Christ.
	Colossians	Paul wrote to correct the false teachings in the church.
	Philemon	Paul wrote to Philemon, whose slave, Onesimus, had robbed him, run away, and met Paul in prison.
	Philippians	Paul thanked the believers for a gift they had recently sent him in prison and to inform of his circumstances.
PAUL'S RELEASE FROM PRISON AD 62	1 Timothy	Paul wrote the three Pastoral Epistles to Timothy and Titus to teach Christian living in response to the gospel.
	Titus	
PAUL'S RETURN TO PRISON AD 64–67?	2 Timothy	

KEY VERSE

For I am not ashamed of the gospel, because it is the power of God for salvation to everyone who believes, first to the Jew, and also to the Greek. For in it the righteousness of God is revealed from faith to faith, just as it is written: The righteous will live by faith.

○

ROMANS 1:16–17

Therefore, just as sin entered the
world through one man, and death through
sin, in this way death spread to all people,
because all sinned. In fact, sin was in the world
before the law, but sin is not charged to a person's
account when there is no law. Nevertheless,
death reigned from Adam to Moses, even over
those who did not sin in the likeness of Adam's
transgression. He is a type of the Coming One.

○

ROMANS 5:12–14

But now, apart from the law, the righteousness of God has been revealed, attested by the Law and the Prophets. The righteousness of God is through faith in Jesus Christ to all who believe, since there is no distinction. For all have sinned and fall short of the glory of God; they are justified freely by his grace through the redemption that is in Christ Jesus. God presented him as the mercy seat by his blood, through faith, to demonstrate his righteousness, because in his restraint God passed over the sins previously committed. God presented him to demonstrate his righteousness at the present time, so that he would be just and justify the one who has faith in Jesus.

○

ROMANS 3:21–26

1-2 Corinthians

Genre | **EPISTLE**

The message of Christ crucified and risen serves as the basis of unity within the church and as the solution for all sins and problems plaguing believers as those whom the Spirit has baptized and gifted (1 Corinthians). The nature of new-covenant ministry patterns itself after the gospel of Jesus: death gives way to life, strength becomes manifest through weakness, and gain comes out of loss (2 Corinthians).

INTRODUCTION

AUTHOR   First Corinthians ascribes Paul as its author (1:1; 16:21). Biblical scholars are almost unanimous that Paul wrote the letter. He wrote it during the last year of his three-year ministry at Ephesus, probably a few weeks before Pentecost in the spring of AD 56 (15:32; 16:8; Acts 20:31). All biblical scholars agree that Paul wrote 2 Corinthians (1:1; 10:1). It contains more personal information about him than any other letter, and its Greek style is especially like that of Romans and 1 Corinthians. Proposed chronologies of Paul's life and ministry include a number of variations. Yet for 2 Corinthians, the consensus is that the letter was written about AD 56 (from Ephesus during Paul's third missionary journey).

BACKGROUND   First Corinthians is the second letter that Paul wrote to the Corinthian church. He had written them an earlier letter, of which no extant copy exists, that included an admonition not to mix with the sexually immoral (5:9). The writing of this second letter (1 Corinthians) was prompted by oral reports from Chloe's household about factional strife within the church (1:11). Although Bible students have often disagreed about the sequence of events that led to the writing of 2 Corinthians, the following scenario seems likely. First Corinthians was not well received by the church at Corinth. As a result, Paul later wrote a (now lost) severe letter of stinging rebuke to Corinth from Ephesus (2 Cor 2:3–4,9). He sent this letter by Titus. Titus came to Paul with the news that most of the Corinthian church had repented. They now accepted Paul's authority (7:5–7). Paul decided to write the Corinthians one more time, expressing his relief but still pleading with an unrepentant minority. He promised to come to Corinth a third time (12:14; 13:1).

MESSAGE AND PURPOSE   Paul's purpose in writing 1 Corinthians was to motivate the Corinthian church to acknowledge the Lord's ownership of them and the implications this had in their lives. Key topics Paul addressed in this overarching theme of the ownership and authority of the Lord include Christian unity, morality, the role of women, spiritual gifts, and the resurrection. Paul wrote to the Corinthian Christians the final time (2 Corinthians) mainly to express his joy that the majority had been restored to him, to ask for an offering on behalf of the poor saints in Jerusalem, and to defend his ministry as an apostle to the minority of unrepentant Corinthian believers. His desire was to encourage the majority and to lead the minority to change its mind about the validity of his apostolic ministry.

SUMMARY   First Corinthians is the most literary of Paul's letters, having a variety of stylistic devices. Paul wanted to communicate to the Corinthians the necessity of accepting the Lord's authority over their lives. Of all Paul's letters, none is more personally revealing of his heart than 2 Corinthians. In it Paul mounts a strong argument ("apology" in the positive sense) for his authority and ministry.

STRUCTURE   Perhaps the most noteworthy feature of the way Paul structured his second letter (1 Corinthians) was his use of the word "about" to introduce a subject. It is apparent that "about" signals that Paul was responding to items on a list of questions that he had received—perhaps by way of a committee of men (16:17). The body of 2 Corinthians is the most disjointed of Paul's letters. It is hard to miss Paul's change of tone from chapters 1–9 (which are warm and encouraging) to chapters 10–13 (which are harsh and threatening). Whatever one decides about the original unity of the letter, no doubt the major turning point of 2 Corinthians occurs at 10:1.

Outlines

1 CORINTHIANS

I.   Greetings and Thanksgiving (1:1–9)

II. Problems in the Church (1:10–6:20)
   A. Divisions and factions (1:10–4:21)
   B. Gross immorality (5:1–13)
   C. Litigation before pagan courts (6:1–11)
   D. Fornication with prostitutes (6:12–20)

III. Replies to Questions from the Corinthians (7:1–14:40)
   A. Questions about marriage (7:1–40)
   B. Limitations of Christian liberty (8:1–11:1)
   C. Veiling of women in public worship (11:2–16)
   D. Disorderly behavior at the Lord's Supper (11:17–34)
   E. Exercise of spiritual gifts (12:1–14:40)

IV. The Resurrection of the Body (15:1–58)
   A. Centrality of Christ's resurrection (15:1–20)
   B. Sequence of resurrection events (15:21–28)
   C. The resurrection and suffering (15:29–34)
   D. Nature of the resurrection body (15:35–49)
   E. The believer's victory over death (15:50–58)

V.   Conclusion (16:1–24)
   A. Collection for the believers at Jerusalem (16:1–4)
   B. Paul's plans for visiting Corinth (16:5–9)
   C. Exhortations, instructions, and salutations (16:10–24)

2 CORINTHIANS

I.   Special Greetings (1:1–11)
   A. Salutation (1:1–2)
   B. Expression of thanksgiving (1:3–11)

II. Clarification of Paul's Ministry (1:12–7:16)
   A. Paul's itinerary explained (1:12–2:4)
   B. Forgiveness and recent travel (2:5–13)
   C. True gospel ministry and doctrinal digression (2:14–7:1)
   D. Paul's joy at receiving good news (7:2–16)

III. A Collection for Needy Christians (8:1–9:15)
   A. Encouragement to generous giving (8:1–15)
   B. Management of the collection (8:16–9:5)
   C. Results of cheerful giving (9:6–15)

IV. The Case against False Apostles (10:1–13:10)
   A. Paul's authority from Christ (10:1–18)
   B. False apostles condemned (11:1–15)
   C. Paul's speech as a fool (11:16–12:10)
   D. Signs of a true apostle (12:11–21)
   E. Basis of Paul's authority (13:1–10)

V.   Final Greetings (13:11–13)

WORD STUDY

sophia

Greek pronunciation:
[sah FEE ah]

CSB translation:
wisdom

Uses in 1 Corinthians: 17
Uses in the NT: 51

Focus passage:
1 Corinthians 2:6

The Greek noun *sophia* means *wisdom, intelligence,* or *knowledge,* but this intelligence and knowledge pertain more to skill in living than to intellectual mastery. Related words are the verb *sophizō,* meaning *to make wise* (2 Tim 3:15; 2 Pet 1:16), and *sophos,* the adjective meaning *wise* or *clever.*

In the OT, *wisdom* refers not to intellectual ability but to one who looks to God for instruction. Solomon stated that "the fear of the LORD is the beginning of knowledge" (Prov 1:7), which implies that even a genius who does not fear God is a fool (see Ps 14:1).

Paul understood *sophia* in the light of the OT. He saw worldly *wisdom* and God's *wisdom* as opposites (see 1 Cor 2:1–9; Col 2:23). The Greeks depended on human mental prowess and insight to unravel the mysteries of life, but Paul relied on God's revelation in Christ (1 Cor 1:30; Eph 1:8–9,17; 3:8–12). This is why Paul said that God's *wisdom* in Christ is not "of this age" and "the *wisdom* of this world is foolishness with God" (1 Cor 2:6; 3:19).

porneia

Greek pronunciation:
[pohr NAY ah]

CSB translation:
sexual immorality

Uses in 1 Corinthians: 5
Uses in the NT: 25

Focus passage:
1 Corinthians 5:1

The Greek noun *porneia* was a general term for all sexual activity outside marriage, so the term can be translated *fornication* or *sexual immorality.* Related terms include *porneuō,* meaning *to commit sexual immorality* (see 1 Cor 6:18); *pornē,* meaning *an immoral woman* or *a female prostitute* (see 6:15–16); and *pornos,* meaning *an immoral person* or *a male prostitute* (5:9–11; 6:9).

Paul condemned a case of incest in the church in Corinth, a sin he called *porneia* (5:1). In chapter 6 he explained that the believer's body is for the Lord and not for *porneia* (v. 13). Then he commanded believers to flee *porneia* (v. 18). On the other hand, sexual union in marriage is commended, partly because it helps believers avoid *porneia* (7:2). It is likely that cult prostitution, in which the Corinthian people could indulge at the temple of Aphrodite, was a major threat to the Corinthian believers' spiritual growth.

sōma

Greek pronunciation:
[SOH mah]

CSB translation:
body

Uses in 1 Corinthians: 46
Uses in the NT: 142

Focus passage:
1 Corinthians 12:12–27

The Greek noun *sōma* means *body* and usually refers to the physical element of a person's existence. The *sōma* needs to be clothed (Matt 6:25), can be killed (Matt 10:28), can be thrown into hell (Matt 5:29–30), can experience resuscitation (Acts 9:40), and will experience resurrection (1 Cor 15:35–44; see Matt 27:52; John 2:19–21). Paul often referred to the *sōma* as the vehicle for sinful actions (Rom 1:24; 6:6,12; 8:10,13; 1 Cor 6:18), but he also used the term figuratively. In Romans 12 the church is "one body in Christ" (v. 5); in 1 Corinthians 12 the church is the "*body* of Christ" (v. 27); in Ephesians and Colossians, the church is the *body* with Christ as its head (Eph 1:22–23; 5:23; Col 1:18; 2:19).

The disunity among the believers in Corinth forced Paul to deal with this problem by expanding at length on the *body* metaphor. Believers in the church are the individual parts that make up Christ's *body.* All parts of Christ's *body* must work together for the *body* to function properly.

1–2 Corinthians Timeline

1000–550 BC

1000
Corinth founded by Dorian Greeks

657–627
Corinth ruled by Cypselus and then his son Periander (627–585)

600
Periander mints Corinthian coins and constructs the Diolkos, a five-foot-wide rock-cut path that ran four miles between two seaports, Lechaion on the Gulf of Corinth and Cenchreae on the Saronic Gulf.

582
The Isthmian games begin and are held every two years to honor Poseidon, the god of the sea.

550
Temple of Apollo constructed

450–27 BC

430
Corinth sides with Sparta and prevails against Athens in the Peloponnesian War.

400
Population of Corinth reaches 100,000

338
Philip II of Macedon conquers Corinth.

336
After Philip II's assassination, the Greeks at the Isthmian games choose Philip's son Alexander the Great to lead them in war with Persia.

146
The Corinthians attempt to resist Roman expansion in Greece and are destroyed by the Roman general Lucius Mummius.

44
Julius Caesar rebuilds Corinth as a colony of Rome, naming it Colonia Laus Julia Corinthiensis.

27
Augustus Caesar makes Corinth the capital of Achaia.

AD 37–50

33
Jesus's trials, death, resurrection, and ascension

33
Pentecost

34
Saul's conversion on the Damascus road

37–40
Paul returns to his native Tarsus.

40
Barnabas travels from Antioch of Syria to find Paul.

47–49
Paul, Barnabas, and John Mark make the first missionary journey.

49–50
Paul and Silas begin second missionary journey by land through Cilicia, Galatia, and Asia Minor to Troas.

50
Paul, Silas, and Timothy sail from Troas to Macedonia and minister in the Macedonian cities of Philippi, Thessalonica, and Berea.

50
Paul preaches on Mars Hill in Athens.

AD 50–57

50–51
Paul arrives in Corinth and spends 18 months planting the church.

51
Paul meets Aquila and Priscilla, who had come to Corinth when Emperor Claudius expelled the Jews from Rome six years earlier.

51
Paul writes 1 and 2 Thessalonians from Corinth.

51
Paul's hearing before Corinth's preconsul, Gallio, brother of the Roman philosopher Seneca

53
Paul begins his third missionary journey by land through Asia Minor to Ephesus.

53–56
Paul writes 1 Corinthians from Ephesus.

54–56
Paul writes 2 Corinthians from Ephesus.

57
Paul spends the winter in Corinth, from where he writes Romans.

57
Paul returns to Jerusalem with funds he had collected from Gentile churches to support the poor in the Jerusalem church.

Paul's List of Spiritual Gifts

NOTE: This list is numbered by the order in which each gift appears within the individual Scripture passages.

SPIRITUAL GIFT	ROMANS 12:6-8	1 CORINTHIANS 12:8-10	1 CORINTHIANS 12:28	1 CORINTHIANS 12:29-30	EPHESIANS 4:11
Apostle			1	1	1
Prophet	1	5	2	2	2
Teacher	3		3	3	5
Pastor					4
Miracles		4	4	4	
Discernment of Spirits		6			
Word of Wisdom/ Knowledge		1			
Evangelists					3
Exhorters	4				
Faith		2			
Healings		3	5	5	
Tongues		7	8	6	
Interpretation		8		7	
Ministry/Serving	2				
Leading	6		7		
Helpers			6		
Mercy	7				
Giving	5				

References to the Lord's Supper

LORD'S SUPPER

A memorial celebrated by the early church to signify Jesus's sacrificial death for humankind's sin. The form of the observance was established by the Lord at the Last Supper when he symbolically offered himself as the Lamb of atonement. His actual death the next day fulfilled the prophecy. Only Paul used the phrase "Lord's Supper" (1 Cor 11:20), although implication of it is made in Revelation 19:9 ("marriage feast of the Lamb"). Church groups celebrate the Lord's Supper regularly as a sign of the new covenant sealed by Christ's death and resurrection.

FELLOWSHIP

Immediately after Paul spoke of "sharing in the body of Christ" through participation in the Lord's Supper (1 Cor 10:16), he said, "Because there is one bread, we who are many are one body" (1 Cor 10:17). This illustrates clearly Paul's belief that fellowship with Christ was to issue into fellowship between believers. Once we grasp this, it is easy to understand why Paul was so angry over the mockery that the Corinthians were making of the Lord's Supper.

EUCHARIST

Church fathers began to call the occasion the "Eucharist" (that is, "Thanksgiving") from the blessing pronounced over the bread and cup after about AD 100.

COMMUNION

The tendency of many Christians to refer to the Lord's Supper as "communion" is rooted in Paul's use of the term *koinonia* in the context of his descriptions of the Lord's Supper. He described the cup as "sharing in the blood of Christ" and the bread as "sharing in the body of Christ" (1 Cor 10:16).

Resurrection Appearances in Scripture

"For I passed on to you as most important what I also received: that Christ died for our sins according to the Scriptures, that he was buried, that he was raised on the third day according to the Scriptures, and that he appeared to Cephas, then to the Twelve. Then he appeared to over five hundred brothers and sisters at one time; most of them are still alive, but some have fallen asleep. Then he appeared to James, then to all the apostles. Last of all, as to one born at the wrong time, he also appeared to me" (1 Cor 15:3–8).

The bodily, living appearance of Jesus of Nazareth after he died and was buried provided certain hope for the resurrection of believers.

Because of Jesus's standing again from the dead, resurrection has come to mean the restoration of the whole self by God, who gave life and creates it anew in the heavenly kingdom. New Testament accounts of the resurrection fall into three categories: the empty tomb, appearances of Jesus before his ascension, and appearances of Jesus after his ascension. Below are those to whom Jesus appeared after his resurrection and before his ascension.

CEPHAS	Also known as Simon Peter	Luke 24:34
THE TWELVE	The disciples	Luke 24:36–43
THE 500	Supposed by some to refer to the ascension	Acts 1:9–11; 1 Cor 15:6
JAMES	Believed to be James, the brother of Jesus	Acts 15:13
THE APOSTLES	Jesus presented himself to Thomas a week after the first appearance to the apostles.	John 20:24–29
PAUL	Jesus spoke to Paul on the road to Damascus.	Acts 9:1–9

Problems in Corinth

Paul dealt with several problems in his first letter to the Corinthians. He learned of these matters through the report from Chloe's people, common rumors, and information received from the church. Paul addressed these problems:

Those Who Bring Division in the Church

HUMAN PRIDE — Some were claiming to follow Paul, Apollos, or Cephas (Peter), and others followed Christ himself (1:12). The gospel message originated not in profound human thought but in the Holy Spirit.

INFANTS IN CHRIST — The Corinthian church showed a great misunderstanding of the essential truth of the gospel. The Corinthians evidenced a wrong concept of wisdom (1:18–2:5), a wrong concept of the gospel (2:6–13), and a wrong concept of spirituality (2:14–3:4).

The Treatment of Fellow Christians Living in Sin

IMMORALITY — Paul had heard reports of sexual immorality among the church (5:1). The Corinthians had done nothing to deal with the issue. Paul urged them to discipline the man by expelling him from the church, severing his connection with God's people.

THE SPIRIT'S TEMPLE IN OUR BODY — Sexual relations outside marriage are a perversion of the divinely established marriage union. Believers have been bought by Christ. The body is a temple of the Holy Spirit. Christians must glorify God in their bodies (6:9–20).

Matters of Sexuality in Marriage and Divorce

Paul maintained marriage as the normal rule of life. He offered general principles for marriage (7:1–7). He then gave advice to the unmarried (7:8–9), to the married (7:10–11), to the separated (7:11), for when an unbeliever abandons a believer (7:12–16), about contentment (7:17–24), and to virgins and widows (7:25–35).

Propriety in Church Worship

THE LORD'S SUPPER — Divisions among the church were magnified through the Lord's Supper instead of seen as a celebration of their unity (10:16–17). Paul exhorted them to examine their motives, methods, and manners as they gathered for the Lord's Supper.

Disputes about Food

MEAT — Most meat available in the marketplace came from sacrificed animals. Some Christians felt that because they were convinced that no idols had reality (8:6), the food was still fit to eat. Yet love, not knowledge, is the key to Christian conduct (8:1–13). It would be better not to eat meat than to lead a fellow believer into sin.

CHRISTIAN DISCIPLINE — Paul stressed that one should subordinate one's own interests to those of others, especially those of Christ and his gospel (9:1–23). No matter how long one has been a Christian, it is a life of discipline, not license, that is important (9:24–27).

IDOLATRY — Paul warned the Corinthians not to grumble or to dabble with idolatry (10:6–12). Christians, however, need not be fearful in the face of temptation, for God will provide help and a way of escape for those who choose to take it (10:13).

CHRISTIAN FREEDOM — Summarizing the discussion, Paul explained that it was not that the meat had been contaminated but that weak Christians can taint their consciences. Believers must always act in a spirit of love and self-discipline, with the good of the community in mind and God's glory in focus.

Spiritual Gifts

JESUS IS LORD — All spiritual gifts are given by the Spirit. No one speaking by the Spirit's power will use derogatory words about Jesus.

GIFTS OF THE SPIRIT — Paul identified nine gifts of the Spirit (12:4–31a). Despite any talents Christians may have, if love is not present, they are of no value (13:1–3). Gifts should be used to strengthen the church (14:26).

The Resurrection

Paul pointed out that if the Corinthians did not maintain their view of Jesus's resurrection, the work of proclaiming the hope that comes from the gospel would be in vain (15:1–34). And one day, thanks to the victory of Christ, death finally will be abolished (15:52–57).

"The Lord Who Is the Spirit": The Trinity in 1–2 Corinthians

TRINITARIAN EXPRESSION	PASSAGES
Trinitarian Greeting *Both the Father and the Son are mentioned as the source of grace and peace, indicating the two divine persons are equal and distinct.*	"Grace to you and peace from God our Father and the Lord Jesus Christ." *(1 Cor 1:3)*
Trinitarian Calling, Fellowship, and Perseverance *God the Father's faithfulness is the ground for the Corinthian believers' ability to endure to the end because he called them into fellowship and union with his Son, Jesus, our Lord.*	"He will also strengthen you to the end, so that you will be blameless in the day of our Lord Jesus Christ. God is faithful; you were called by him into fellowship with his Son, Jesus Christ our Lord." *(1 Cor 1:8–9)*
Trinitarian Monotheism *In this allusion to the sacred Shema that Jews recited daily (Deut 6:4), the Father is identified with the one true God of Israel and Jesus is identified with this same God, the Lord. God the Father and Jesus, the Son, are distinct yet seen as equal with the one true God.*	"'There is no God but one.' For even if there are so-called gods, whether in heaven or on earth—as there are many 'gods' and many 'lords'—yet for us there is one God, the Father. All things are from him, and we exist for him. And there is one Lord, Jesus Christ. All things are through him, and we exist through him." *(1 Cor 8:4b–6; cp. Deut 6:4)*
Trinitarian Profession of Faith *The Holy Spirit enables believers to confess that Jesus is Lord.*	"Therefore I want you to know that no one speaking by the Spirit of God says, 'Jesus is cursed,' and no one can say, 'Jesus is Lord,' except by the Holy Spirit." *(1 Cor 12:3)*
Trinitarian Life and Salvation *Christ's work and the Holy Spirit's work in salvation are closely related in giving believers eternal life, so much so that Christ, the last Adam, can be called "a life-giving spirit" and the Lord identified with the Spirit.*	"So it is written, The first man Adam became a living being; the last Adam became a life-giving spirit [or Spirit]." *(1 Cor 15:45; cp. Gen 2:7)* "We all, with unveiled faces, are looking as in a mirror at the glory of the Lord and are being transformed into the same image from glory to glory; this is from the Lord who is the Spirit." *(2 Cor 3:18)*

Galatians

Genre | **EPISTLE**

Because Jesus the Messiah has delivered them from this present evil age, the people of God are no longer defined by keeping the law but instead are justified by faith in the Messiah and have been enabled to lead righteous lives in the Spirit.

INTRODUCTION

AUTHOR The author's name is "Paul," and he claims to be "an apostle" of Christ (Gal 1:1). The autobiographical information in the letter is consistent with what is known about the apostle Paul from Acts and his other letters. Theologically, everything in Galatians agrees with Paul's views elsewhere, notably in Romans.

BACKGROUND A key consideration is comparing the basis of contention in Galatians to the topic of debate at the Jerusalem Council. The problem addressed in Galatians is that "the works of the law" of Moses (2:16–17; 3:2; cp. 5:4), notably circumcision (5:2; 6:12–13), were added by some teachers to what was required to be justified before God. This is the same issue that Acts records as the reason why the Jerusalem Council met (Acts 15:1,5), supporting the idea that the existing problem in the Galatian churches was part of the reason for the Jerusalem Council. If Galatians was written after the Jerusalem Council, it is inconceivable that Paul would not have cited the conclusions of the council, which supported his works-free view of the gospel. This strongly implies that the Jerusalem Council had not yet occurred when Paul wrote Galatians.

MESSAGE AND PURPOSE Galatians was written to clarify and defend "the truth of the gospel" (2:5,14) in the face of a false gospel. This was done by (1) defending Paul's message and authority as an apostle, (2) considering the Old Testament basis of the gospel message, and (3) demonstrating how the gospel message Paul preached worked practically in daily Christian living. Paul chose this approach to correct those in the Galatian churches in regard to both their faith and their practice related to the gospel.

SUMMARY Galatians, which may be the earliest of Paul's letters, is also his most impassioned. It gives us a strong presentation of the truth that sinners are justified and live godly lives by trusting in Jesus alone.

STRUCTURE Galatians follows the typical pattern for a first-century letter, with the exception of the element of thanksgiving: a salutation (1:1–5), the main body (1:6–6:15), and a farewell (6:16–18). Contrasting concepts are prominent in the letter: divine revelation vs. human insight, grace vs. law, justification vs. condemnation, Jerusalem vs. Mount Sinai, sonship vs. slavery, the fruit of the Spirit vs. the works of the flesh, and liberty vs. bondage.

Outline

WORD STUDY

peritomē

Greek pronunciation:
[peh ree tah MAY]

CSB translation:
circumcision

Uses in Galatians: 7
Uses in the NT: 36

Focus passage:
Galatians 2:7–21

The Greek noun **peritomē** means *circumcision,* and the related verb *peritemnō* means *to circumcise,* occurring 17 times in the NT. These two terms refer to the practice of cutting off the foreskin of a male, normally at birth. God chose *circumcision* as a special sign of the relationship between himself and the covenant people of Israel, starting with Abraham (Gen 17:9–14,22–27).

In Paul's writings, *peritomē* is prominently used in relation to salvation. Some Jewish believers claimed that Gentiles must be *circumcised* and follow the law of Moses to be saved (see Acts 15:1–35). Paul explained that this was not true of their father Abraham, for he lived before the law of Moses and was declared righteous before he was *circumcised. Circumcision* made no contribution to Abraham's relationship with God; that relationship was based on faith (Rom 4:9–25). Both the *circumcised* and the *uncircumcised* are saved by faith (Rom 3:30; see Gal 5:6,11; 6:15).

nomos

Greek pronunciation:
[NAH mahss]

CSB translation:
law

Uses in Galatians: 32
Uses in the NT: 194

Focus passage:
Galatians 3:2–26

The Greek noun **nomos** means *custom, ordinance,* or *law.* In the Greek OT, *nomos* is used to translate the Hebrew term *torah* 247 times, where it normally refers to the law of Moses in general or to specific *laws.* Over half of its occurrences in the NT are in Paul's writings.

In Romans and Galatians, Paul fought the battle over *law* and grace in relation to salvation. Paul's phrase "the works of the law" (Gal 3:2) refers to the idea of a salvation based on keeping the *law.* Paul denied that a *law-based* righteousness, which is dependent on human effort instead of God's grace and faith in Christ's work, can save or sustain anyone. The *law* brings the knowledge of sin and makes everyone accountable to God (Rom 3:19–20; Gal 3:15–22). By showing unbelievers their sinfulness, the *law* acts as their guardian until they trust in Christ through faith and become sons of God (Gal 3:23–26).

huios

Greek pronunciation:
[hwee AHSS]

CSB translation:
son

Uses in Galatians: 13
Uses in the NT: 377

Focus passage:
Galatians 4:4–7

The Greek noun **huios** means *son,* referring to male offspring (Matt 1:21; 20:20). The two most common uses of *huios* in the NT are in titles for Christ and designations for believers. The expressions "*Son*" and "*Son of God*" refer to Christ in his unique and eternal relationship with the Father (Matt 3:17; 8:29; 11:27; John 3:16–18,35–36; 5:19–27; 8:36; 14:13; 17:1; Rom 1:3–4; 8:29,32; Heb 1:2,5,8). However, "*Son of God*" is also used many times as a messianic title (Matt 14:33; 16:16; 26:63; Mark 1:1; John 1:34,49; 11:27; 20:31), as is "*Son of David*" (Matt 9:27; 12:23; 15:22; 20:30–31; 21:9,15; 22:42,45). Jesus's self-designation "*Son of Man*" is a messianic title taken from Daniel 7:13–14 (Matt 8:20; 12:8; 19:28; 24:47; 25:31; 26:64; John 1:51). On the basis of Jesus's sonship, believers are called *sons* (Gal 4:6–7) and "*sons* of God" (Matt 5:9; Rom 8:14,19; Gal 3:26). Their adoption into God's family places them in a special relationship to God so that they can call him "*Abba,* Father" and enjoy an inheritance (Gal 4:4–7).

Galatians & James Timeline

300 BC–AD 35

278 BC
The Galatians, Celts of European origins, invade Asia Minor.

63–36 BC
Mark Antony and Pompey reward the Galatians with additional territory for supporting Rome in its wars against Mithridates.

25 BC
Amyntas, king of Galatia, wills his kingdom to Rome at his death.

AD 33
Jesus's trials, death, resurrection, and ascension

AD 33
Following his resurrection, Jesus appears to James, his half-brother.

AD 33
Pentecost

AD 34
Saul's conversion on the Damascus road

AD 36–45

37?
Paul meets with Peter and James on his first visit to Jerusalem following his conversion.

37–40
Paul returns to his native Tarsus.

40
Barnabas travels from Antioch of Syria to find Paul.

41
Barnabas and Paul serve together in Antioch.

41
Claudius succeeds Caligula as emperor.

44
James, Jesus's half-brother, becomes leader of the church at Jerusalem.

AD 46–49

46
Judea experiences severe famine.

47–49
Paul, Barnabas, and John Mark make their first missionary journey.

48–52
The Letter of James

49
From Syrian Antioch, Paul writes his letter to the Galatians, assuming the destination of the letter was the churches of southern Galatia: Iconium, Lystra, and Derbe.

49
Barnabas and Paul travel from Antioch to Jerusalem for the conference dealing with the question of whether Gentiles had to be circumcised in order to be saved.

49
Paul and Barnabas part ways over the question of whether John Mark should be allowed to join them on a second missionary journey.

AD 49–51

49
Paul and Silas team up for an overland journey to revisit cities of south Galatia as the first segment of Paul's second missionary journey.

49
Timothy joins Paul and Silas as they travel through north Galatia to Troas.

50
Paul, Silas, and Timothy sail from Troas to Macedonia, planting the church in Philippi.

50
Paul and his companions move from Philippi to Thessalonica and Berea.

50–51
As a result of much persecution, Paul and his companions split up, with Paul going to Corinth by way of Athens.

AD 60–330

62
Martyrdom of James, half-brother of Jesus

70
Destruction of Jerusalem

230
Origen quotes James in his commentary on the Gospel of John.

330
Eusebius refers to the Letter of James as Scripture.

First-Century Heresies

First-century heresies threatened unity within the body of Christ as Christianity
spread through Jewish and Hellenistic cultures.

LEGALISM

On one end of the spectrum is the belief in strict adherence to the law—that one must con-
tinually try to follow the law perfectly in order to be in God's good graces and maintain salvation. Yet the Bible tells us that God made an unalterable promise to raise those who believe in
Jesus to an eternity in heaven. Once people have been "justified by faith" (Rom 5:1), having
received the Spirit as God's pledge of love (Rom 5:5; 8:35,39), then they can rest assured that
they are saved by grace. The Christian hope for the future is grounded in the faithfulness of
God, not in our ability to follow the law.

ANTINOMIANISM

On the other end of the spectrum, antinomianism is the false teaching that since faith
alone is necessary for salvation, one is free from the moral obligations of the law. The word
antinomianism is not used in the Bible, but the idea is spoken of. Paul appears to have been
falsely accused of being an antinomian: "What should we say then? Should we continue in sin
so that grace may multiply?" (Rom 6:1; see also Rom 3:8; 6:15). While it is true that obedience
to the law will never earn salvation for anyone (Eph 2:8–9), it is equally true that those who
are saved are expected to live a life full of good works: "Watch out, brothers and sisters, so that
there won't be in any of you an evil, unbelieving heart that turns away from the living God"
(Heb 3:12; see also Matt 7:16–20; Eph 2:10; Col 1:10; Jas 2:14–26). It's possible to stray from
grace, deserting the core principles of participating in the abundant life that Jesus desires for
his followers. Since we have been freed from the dominion of sin through faith in Jesus, we have
also been freed to practice the righteousness demanded by God: "For in Christ Jesus neither
circumcision nor uncircumcision accomplishes anything; what matters is faith working through
love. . . . What matters instead is a new creation" (Gal 5:6; 6:15; see also Rom 6:12–22).

GNOSTICISM

The term *gnosticism* is derived from the Greek word *gnosis* (knowledge) because secret knowledge was a crucial doctrine of Gnosticism. Although wide variations existed among the many
gnostic sects, certain major features were common to most gnostics: the separation of an inferior god who was responsible for creation and the superior god revealed as Jesus the Redeemer
(1 John 1:1–2); the division of Christians into categories with one group being the superior,
higher class than ordinary Christians because they had received a divine spark as the elect of
the good deity (Gal 1:6–7); the stress on secret teachings that only divine persons could com-
prehend, as only this secret knowledge could awaken the divine spark within the elect (1 John
5:1–13); and the belief that faith was inferior to knowledge, a self-discovery experience that
claimed to solve life's mysteries and was enhanced by participation in rituals (see Acts 4:12;
Col 2:18).

Works vs. Fruit

WORKS OF THE FLESH

The works of the flesh are obvious throughout Scripture and life and often overlap. For example, the Israelites in the wilderness worshipped their golden calf with sacrifices and revelry (Exod 32:1–6).

FRUIT OF THE SPIRIT

The fruit of the Spirit grows not by exerting our own strength but by walking in the Spirit. These virtues grow out of our relationship with God (Gal 5:22–23).

SEX (GAL 5:19)

Sexual Immorality ... General term for all forms of sexual sin

Moral Impurity .... Often denotes sexual sin

Promiscuity .... Emphasizes lack of restraint, unbridled passions

RELIGION (V. 20)

Idolatry .... Worshipping created things instead of Creator God

Sorcery .... Trying to manipulate circumstances or dark powers

RELATIONSHIPS (VV. 20–21)

Hatreds .... Enmity of any kind

Strife .... Having a contentious temper

Jealousy .... Wanting what someone else possesses

Outbursts of Anger .. An uncontrolled temper

Selfish Ambitions .... Selfish, impure motives

Dissensions .... A spirit of dividing from others

Factions .... A "party spirit" leading to divisions

Envy .... Discontent with God's gifts and the success of others

INDULGENCES (V. 21)

Drunkenness .... Inability to control one's appetite for alcohol

Carousing .... Inability to control one's appetite for pleasure

ANYTHING SIMILAR (V. 21)

LOVE	Paul says "fruit," not "fruits." Collectively, these qualities, or attributes, make up Christlikeness. Being conformed into the image of Jesus means embodying the fruit of the Spirit more and more.
JOY	
PEACE	
PATIENCE	
KINDNESS	
GOODNESS	
FAITHFULNESS	
GENTLENESS	
SELF-CONTROL	

You who are trying to be justified by the law are alienated from Christ; you have fallen from grace. For we eagerly await through the Spirit, by faith, the hope of righteousness. For in Christ Jesus neither circumcision nor uncircumcision accomplishes anything; what matters is faith working through love.

○

GALATIANS 5:4–6

Ephesians

Genre | **EPISTLE**

God's plan to display Jesus the Messiah's universal lordship
through his reconciling sinners to God entails
the reconciliation of sinners, Jew and Gentile, with one
another and the willful living out of these new-creational
realities by those united to Christ by faith.

INTRODUCTION

AUTHOR Paul referred to himself by name as the author of the book of Ephesians in two places (1:1; 3:1). Many regard this book as the crown of all of Paul's writings. In line with the indisputable acceptance of Pauline authorship in the early church, there is no reason to dispute the Pauline authorship of Ephesians.

BACKGROUND Paul penned the letter while in prison (3:1; 4:1; 6:20). Disagreement exists concerning whether Paul was imprisoned in Caesarea (Acts 24:22) around AD 57–59 or in Rome (Acts 28:30) in about 60–62 when he wrote this letter. Tradition suggests that Paul wrote the letter from Rome around AD 60–61, which would have transpired while Paul was under house arrest in guarded rental quarters (Acts 28:30). Paul most likely wrote Colossians, Philemon, and Philippians during the same imprisonment.

MESSAGE AND PURPOSE Central to the message of Ephesians is the re-creation of the human family according to God's original intention for it. The new creation destroys the misguided view that God accepts the Jew and rejects the Gentile. Paul says the distinction was abolished at Christ's sacrificial death. Thus no more hindrance remains to reuniting all humanity as the people of God, with Christ as the head (1:22–23). The new body, the church, has been endowed by the power of the Holy Spirit to enable them to live out their new lives (1:3–2:10) and put into practice the new standards (4:1–6:9). In sum, we can say that the overall emphasis of Ephesians is on the unity of the church in Christ through the power of the Spirit.

SUMMARY Paul's letter to the Ephesians is an anthem to the sovereign grace of God displayed toward sinners in Christ. It contains some of the worst news ("you were dead in your trespasses and sins," 2:9) and best news ("but God . . . made us alive with Christ," 2:4–5) in all of Scripture. In view of this grace, Paul calls believers to "walk worthy of the calling" we have received (4:1).

STRUCTURE The salutation and structure of Ephesians are quite similar to Colossians. Many topics are commonly treated in both letters. The message is strikingly similar. Of the 155 verses in Ephesians, over half contain identical expressions to those in Colossians. Colossians, however, is abrupt, argumentative, and seemingly compressed. Ephesians presents a bigger, finished picture that is meditative, instructive, and expansive.

Outline

I. **Introduction (1:1–14)**
   A. Greetings (1:1–2)
   B. God's purposes in Christ (1:3–14)

II. **Paul's Prayer of Thanksgiving (1:15–23)**

III. **Salvation by Grace through Faith (2:1–10)**

IV. **Unity of God's New People (2:11–22)**

V. **Revelation of the Divine Mystery (3:1–13)**

VI. **Paul's Prayer for Strength and Love (3:14–21)**

VII. **Unity of the Body of Christ (4:1–16)**
   A. Exhortation to unity (4:1–6)
   B. The variety of gifts (4:7–12)
   C. The maturity of the church (4:13–16)

VIII. **Exhortations to Holy Living (4:17–5:21)**

IX. **New Relationships (5:22–6:9)**
   A. Wives and husbands (5:22–33)
   B. Children and parents (6:1–4)
   C. Slaves and masters (6:5–9)

X. **Warfare of the New People (6:10–20)**

XI. **Conclusion (6:21–24)**

proorizō

Greek pronunciation:
[prah ah RID zoh]

CSB translation:
predestine

Uses in Ephesians: 2
Uses in the NT: 6

Focus passage:
Ephesians 1:5,11

Proorizō (*predestine, predetermine*) first appears in Greek literature in the writings of Paul, who may have coined the term. In the NT, this verb consistently refers to God's *predetermined* plan to culminate salvation history in the person of Jesus Christ. For this reason, God the Father is always the subject of this verb in the NT. The early church saw Jesus's sufferings as the *predetermined* plan of God in accordance with OT Scriptures (Acts 4:28). The whole of the Christian salvation experience has been *predestined* by God. Christians have received both their calling and adoption into the rights of Christian sonship because of God's loving *predetermination* (Rom 8:30; Eph 1:5,11). God has *predetermined* those whom he foreknew (see *proginōskō*; Rom 11:2) to be ultimately conformed to the image of his Son, Jesus (Rom 8:29). Finally, God *predetermined* before the ages his mysterious plan of salvation (1 Cor 2:7).

apolutrōsis

Greek pronunciation:
[ah pah LEW troh sihs]

CSB translation:
redemption

Uses in Ephesians: 3
Uses in the NT: 10

Focus passage:
Ephesians 1:7,14; 4:30

In the NT, **apolutrōsis** may refer to present or future *redemption*. When referring to future *redemption*, the term looks to the salvation of the Christian's physical body from the distresses of this world. The Son of Man's return will usher in release from suffering and persecution (Luke 21:28). In Paul's theology, the future *redemption* of our physical bodies will be accompanied both by the church's full adoption into divine sonship and by the creation being set free from decay (Rom 8:18–23). Presently, the Holy Spirit is the down payment guaranteeing the future "*redemption* of the possession" (meaning God will fully *redeem* his church and/or the church will posses its full inheritance; Eph 1:14; 4:30). Christians have *redemption*, described as the forgiveness of sins (Eph 1:7; Col 1:14). Thus the work of God in Christ ensures both present and future *redemption* for his people.

rhēma

Greek pronunciation:
[HRAY mah]

CSB translation:
word

Uses in Ephesians: 2
Uses in the NT: 68

Focus passage:
Ephesians 6:17

Rhēma most frequently appears in the narrative literature of the four Gospels and Acts (a total of 52 times). In the NT, *rhēma* (*word*) is used with two different senses. The term is first used with the sense of *that which is said or expressed*. Here the word focuses on what has been communicated. For example, Jesus speaks of men having to give account for every careless *word* they speak (Matt 12:36). In this sense, *rhēma* may also refer to any one of many different types of communication. For example, *rhēma* can refer to a *prophecy* or *prediction* (e.g., Mark 9:32), to a *speech* or *sermon* (e.g., Rom 10:18), to the *gospel* or a *confessional statement* (e.g., 1 Pet 1:25), or to a *commandment* or *order* (e.g., Heb 11:3). However, *rhēma* does not always focus on what has been communicated. It may refer simply to a *thing*, an *object*, a *matter*, or an *event*. For example, both Jesus (Matt 18:16) and Paul (2 Cor 13:1) quote Deuteronomy to the effect that every *fact* must be confirmed by the testimony of two or three witnesses.

Ephesians Timeline

1400–450 BC

1400–1300
Ephesus is first occupied.

1000
Greeks cross the Aegean Sea and settle in Ephesus.

561
Croesus, king of Lydia, captures Ephesus.

560
Temple of the moon goddess, Artemis, is funded and built by Croesus.

540–480
Heraclitus of Ephesus, an early philosopher

450–85 BC

JULY 21, 356
Herostratus burns the temple of Artemis to establish his place in history.

323–281
A 25,000-seat stadium is built in Ephesus during the reign of Lysimachus.

280–133
Ephesus is under the control of the Seleucids and the Ptolemies.

133
Ephesus comes under Roman control when King Attalus III of Pergamum wills his kingdom to Rome and the Roman province of Asia is created.

89
The Ephesians rebel against Roman taxation, looking to Mithridates VI Eupator, king of Pontus, as liberator. A large number of Italians are killed in the rebellion.

50 BC–AD 54

33–32 BC
Mark Antony and Cleopatra reside in Ephesus.

AD 17
Ephesus experiences a destructive earthquake.

AD 52
Paul travels through Ephesus toward the end of his second missionary journey.

AD 52
Apollos comes to Ephesus and is mentored by Aquila and Priscilla.

AD 54
Paul returns to Ephesus for a two-and-a-half-year ministry.

AD 55–110

56
Paul writes 1 Corinthians from Ephesus.

61
Paul writes his letter to the Ephesians.

62
Timothy, bishop of Ephesus, receives his first letter from Paul.

67
Timothy receives his second letter from Paul.

67?
Paul's death in Rome

110
Ignatius of Antioch sends one of his seven letters to the church at Ephesus.

Mystery in the New Testament

The New Testament uses the word for "mystery" about 25 times, once in the Gospels (Mark 4:11; cp. Matt 13:11; Luke 8:10), 21 times in Paul's writings, and a few times in Revelation. The term has several facets, but it is clear that the New Testament usage differs from that of the mystery religions.

The mystery of the New Testament has been described as an "open secret"; matters previously kept secret in God's eternal purposes have now been or are being revealed (1 Cor 2:7–8; Eph 3:3–5). In contrast to the mystery religions, the mystery of the New Testament appears in the historical activity of the person of Christ: "He made known to us the mystery of his will, according to his good pleasure that he purposed in Christ" (Eph 1:9; see also Col 2:2); the indwelling Christ is "the hope of glory" (Col 1:26–27).

The mystery is received spiritually (Eph 3:4–5) and manifested in the proclamation of the gospel (Eph 6:19). Part of the mystery involves the disclosure that Gentiles share in the blessings of the gospel: "At that time you were without Christ, excluded from the citizenship of Israel, and foreigners to the covenants of promise, without hope and without God in the world. But now in Christ Jesus, you who were far away have been brought near by the blood of Christ" (Eph 2:12–13).

Armor in Ephesians

In Ephesians 6:10–17, the apostle Paul provided his readers with a vivid description of the appearance of a legionary's armor:

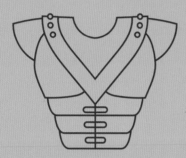

- Paul's depiction of Roman armor corresponds very well with what we otherwise know about legionary battle dress in his time. In this passage, he compared the equipment of the legionary to "the full armor of God" (vv. 11,13) as an illustration of the Christian's need to remain steadfast in opposing every form of evil.

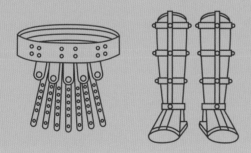

- Verses 14–17 list six items of military armor in this order: girdle (waist belt) and breastplate (*lorica segmentata*), shoes and shield, helmet and sword. Note the absence of the javelin and greaves, items that had been dropped from the legionary's standard equipment by Paul's day. Paul seems to have listed the items of armor roughly in the order in which they would be donned or taken up by the soldier.

- He told the readers to stand firm in the faith (v. 13), just as the legionary's sandals were designed for firm footing. Satan, the Christian warrior's enemy, fights from a distance, hurling "flaming arrows" (v. 16). The Christian's shield, like the Roman legionary's, is designed not merely to block these flaming missiles but to "extinguish" them (v. 16). As a signal that the battle with evil is imminent, the Christian dons his "helmet of salvation" and draws his "sword of the Spirit—which is the word of God" (v. 17).

- Paul's description of Roman armor as a metaphor for the Christian's struggle against evil is one of the most memorable passages in all his letters. In this portrait of the believer's spiritual struggle, he has given the faithful of all ages the courage to face the evil one with confidence and assurance of victory.

Dead in Sin, Alive in Christ

DEAD IN SIN	ALIVE IN CHRIST
"You were dead in your trespasses and sins." *(Eph 2:1)*	"God . . . made us alive with Christ even though we were dead in trespasses." *(Eph 2:4–5)*
"You previously walked according to the ways of this world." *(Eph 2:2)*	"We are [God's] workmanship, created in Christ Jesus for good works, which God prepared ahead of time for us to [walk in]." *(Eph 2:10)*
"You previously walked . . . according to the ruler of the power of the air, the spirit now working in the disobedient." *(Eph 2:2)*	"In the coming ages [God] might display the immeasurable riches of his grace through his kindness to us in Christ Jesus." *(Eph 2:7)*
"We were by nature children under wrath." *(Eph 2:3)*	"You are saved by grace! . . . This is not from your-selves; it is God's gift—not from works, so that no one can boast." *(Eph 2:5,8b–9)*
"We too all previously lived among them in our fleshly desires, carrying out the inclinations of our flesh and thoughts." *(Eph 2:3a)*	"He also raised us up with him and seated us with him in the heavens in Christ Jesus." *(Eph 2:6)*

Union with Christ: Past, Present, and Future

RAISED WITH CHRIST (PAST)	HIDDEN WITH CHRIST (PRESENT)	GLORIFIED WITH CHRIST (FUTURE)
"If you have been raised with Christ, seek the things above, where Christ is, seated at the right hand of God." *(Col 3:1)*	"For you died, and your life is hidden with Christ in God." *(Col 3:3)*	"When Christ, who is your life, appears, then you also will appear with him in glory." *(Col 3:4)*

Philippians

Genre | **EPISTLE**

The path to joyful Christian fellowship is found in seeking others' interests above our own, which was shown principally in Jesus's coming in the form of a servant who suffered and later would be exalted.

INTRODUCTION

AUTHOR

Paul the apostle wrote this short letter, a fact that no scholar seriously questions.

BACKGROUND

The traditional date for the writing of Philippians is during Paul's first Roman imprisonment (AD 60–62); few have challenged this conclusion. Paul planted the church at Philippi during his second missionary journey (AD 50) in response to his "Macedonian vision" (Acts 16:9–10). This was the first church in Europe (Acts 16). The text of this letter from Paul suggests several characteristics of the church at Philippi. First, Gentiles predominated. Few Jews lived in Philippi, and apparently, the church had few. Second, women had a significant role (Acts 16:11–15; Phil 4:1–2). Third, the church was generous. Fourth, they remained deeply loyal to Paul.

MESSAGE AND PURPOSE

One purpose of this letter was for Paul to explain his situation at Rome (1:12–26). Although he was concerned about the divided Christian community at Rome, his outlook was strengthened by the knowledge that Christ was being magnified. Paul's theology of life formed the basis of his optimism. Whether he lived or died, whether he continued his service to others or went to be in Christ's presence, or whether he was appreciated or not, he wanted Christ to be glorified. Within this explanation are several messages.

SUMMARY

Philippians is Paul's most warmly personal letter. After initial difficulties in the city of Philippi (Acts 16), a strong bond developed between Paul and the converts there. Paul wrote to thank the church for a gift it had recently sent him in prison and to inform them of his circumstances.

STRUCTURE

Philippians can be divided into four primary sections. Paul had definite concerns that he wanted to express, and he also wrote to warn about false teachers who threatened the church. Many of Paul's letters can be divided into theological and practical sections, but Philippians does not follow that pattern. Paul's theological instruction is woven throughout the fabric of a highly personal letter.

Outline

euangelion

Greek pronunciation:
[yoo ahn GEHL ee ahn]

CSB translation:
gospel

Uses in Philippians: 12
Uses in the NT: 76

Focus passage:
Philippians 1:27

The Christian *euangelion* (*gospel*) is the universal good news of God's saving grace through faith in Christ and the message of his kingdom over which Jesus reigns. Jesus preached the *good news* of God's coming kingdom (Matt 4:23) and substantiated his message by miracles (Matt 9:35). The *gospel* of the kingdom's arrival will be preached to the world (Mark 13:10) and is worthy of sacrificial labor (Mark 8:35). Paul believed the *gospel* was an extension of OT promises, where it lay hidden in mystery form (Rom 1:1–3; 16:25–26). Paul's *gospel* encompasses Jesus's entire life: his incarnation, sacrificial death, burial, resurrection, postresurrection appearances, and ascension (Rom 1:1–6; 1 Cor 15:1–8; Phil 2:9). It is the Spirit-empowered message (1 Thess 1:5) by which God calls the elect (2 Thess 2:13–14) and reconciles people to himself (2 Cor 5:18–21). Men will one day be judged by it (Rom 2:16; 2 Thess 1:8).

chairō

Greek pronunciation:
[KIGH roh]

CSB translation:
rejoice

Uses in Philippians: 9
Uses in the NT: 74

Focus passage:
Philippians 4:4

Chairō means *to enjoy a state of gladness, happiness,* or *well-being*. Scripture records numerous events that result in this joyful state: finding something formerly lost (Matt 18:13; Luke 15:5,32), the hope of reward from God (Matt 5:12 = Luke 6:23; Luke 10:20), Jesus's miracles (Luke 13:17; 19:37), his birth (Luke 1:14), his postresurrection appearances (John 20:20), suffering (Acts 5:41; Col 1:24), the repentance of others (2 Cor 7:9), the faith of others (Col 2:5), the preaching about Christ (Phil 1:18), and many other occasions. This act of *rejoicing* in God is commanded for Christians (2 Cor 13:11; Phil 3:1; 4:4; 1 Thess 5:16). *Chairō* was commonly used in Greek to express greetings—whether in written communication (Acts 15:23; 23:26; Jas 1:1) or spoken address (Matt 26:49; 28:9; Luke 1:28).

Paul's Hebrew Heritage

Surely one factor God used was Paul's Jewish heritage. By understanding that heritage, we may better understand how God prepared and used Paul to bless the world. Because synagogues were the power base of the influential sect called the Pharisees, and since Paul called himself a Pharisee ("I am a Pharisee, a son of Pharisees" in Acts 23:6), their influence was profound on Paul's religious education and study of Scripture. Pharisees were the devout, zealous, legalistic students and proponents of Mosaic law. They were Paul's mentors. Gamaliel, one of the most influential Jewish teachers of the day, was Paul's teacher in Jerusalem. Brilliant teachers profoundly influence brilliant students.

In defending himself before the mob in the temple area at the end of the third missionary journey, Paul declared he was "a Jew, born in Tarsus of Cilicia" (Acts 22:3). If "Saul" or "Paul" was a "Jew" and of Hebrew heritage, why did he also have a Roman name like Paul and why did he claim Roman citizenship? A widely held view is that his Hebrew name, Saul, was given at birth and was the name of either his father or some other family member. Another possibility is that his devout parents named him after Israel's first king. After all, King Saul was from the tribe of Benjamin, and Paul declared in Philippians 3:5 that he was "of the tribe of Benjamin."

As to his Roman name, "Paul," many have generally believed he received this at birth because, most likely, his father was a Jew who either purchased Roman citizenship or received it for meritorious service to the empire. Paul clearly claimed his citizenship rights at Philippi when the city magistrates tried to slip him out of town underhandedly. Paul declared, "They beat us in public without a trial, although we are Roman citizens" (Acts 16:37).

When writing Philippians, Paul also declared he had grown up as "a Hebrew born of Hebrews" and "regarding the law, a Pharisee" (Phil 3:5). Thus his childhood had been spent in mastering Jewish Scriptures and sacred traditions. This implies that his family, although living in a Roman and Greek city, spoke Aramaic within the family circle. Paul also would have learned to read the Scriptures in Hebrew in the local synagogue and been able to read and speak Greek (and perhaps even some Latin)!

After receiving years of education from his father at home, Paul would have gone to the synagogue school six days a week from about the age of five or six until he reached the age of twelve or thirteen. A Jewish boy would have spent the morning studying at the school, while in the afternoon he would have returned home to apprentice at a trade such as farming, carpentry, or, in Paul's case, tentmaking (Acts 18:3). At age 12, Paul became a son of the law. At a special ceremony marking the milestone, Paul's father fastened phylacteries (small box-like containers that enclosed the Shema) on his son's left arm and forehead. They symbolized that Paul had learned the law and would live by it and keep it close to his heart to be loved and obeyed.

Paul was probably in his middle to late teens when he went to Jerusalem to study under the most highly respected Jewish teacher of the era—Gamaliel.

Paul first appeared in the New Testament at the stoning of Stephen, which was in Jerusalem sometime after Jesus's death. Saul, the brilliant, zealous defender of Judaism, persecuted the Christian movement because he thought it to be the enemy of his cherished religion and covenant God. When the risen Christ confronted and converted this genius Jew to Christianity, he changed the course of history!

Hymns in the Early Church

The early church was a singing church. In New Testament Scripture we have several references to the songs of early believers:

- Jesus and the disciples sang hymns after the Last Supper (Matt 26:30; Mark 14:26).
- Paul and Silas sang hymns to God while in prison (Acts 16:25).
- Paul's instructions for church order and involvement included allowing those who received a psalm to be free to share in worship. Believers were to sing with the spirit and with understanding (1 Cor 14:15,26).
- Paul encouraged believers to address one another in "psalms, hymns, and spiritual songs" (Eph 5:19; Col 3:16).

The community of believers that formed the nucleus of the early church evolved in the milieu of Jewish culture. They were accustomed to the liturgy and musical practice of the tabernacle and temple. Synagogue worship, which had become a common practice by the New Testament era, included intoning of psalms led by a cantor with congregational participation.

The Hebrew Psalter, Israel's hymnal, was a compilation of psalms from many eras of Israelite history. Members of the Jewish community sang psalms in worship, both personal and corporate. These psalms were comfortable and meaningful. First-century believers who had this Jewish heritage continued using these psalms in worship in the Christian community.

The early Christians knew they needed to tell the story of the Messiah, the Christ. Thus they focused on realities that reflected their own Christian experience in community. They told of God's kingdom, the gospel of grace, carrying the gospel into the world, and the building up of the church.

Many hymns in the New Testament are "Christ hymns." They testify of the work of Christ in coming, dwelling with us, and rising to be with God the Father. One of the best known of the Christ hymns is in Philippians 2:5–11 (for additional Christ hymns, see John 1:1–14; Col 1:15–20; 1 Tim 3:16; Heb 1:1–4; 1 Pet 2:22–24; 3:18–22). The poetic passage was probably part of worship liturgy in that day. This hymn traced salvation's saga. Christ was equal with God yet lowered himself to serve others, even in death. Only then did God exalt him. The church that sang Philippians 2:5–11 knew that, in spite of worldly appearances, all "gods" and "lords" of their contemporary world had been defeated in Jesus Christ.

Certain New Testament passages appear to have the actual literary features of hymn texts. Paul gave direct witness to the use of such hymnic fragments—"psalms, hymns, and spiritual songs" in Colossians 3:16 and its parallel text, Ephesians 5:19–20. Many scholars agree on the following distinctions:

Psalms—Old Testament psalms and canticles or new materials sung in this older style

Hymns—Newly written songs by the Christian community that served as an apology for Christ, worshipping him as Son of God and Savior

Spiritual Songs—Spontaneous outbursts of praise, perhaps improvised singing on the last syllable of the "alleluia."

Scholars who believe interpreters of Scripture should not attach these descriptions support using the term "spiritual" to describe all three terms—psalms, hymns, songs. Neither interpretation takes away from Paul's essential truth. We are to sing from our hearts to God. Rather than vain recitation, it is to be a matter of personal devotion.

KEY VERSE

Rejoice in the Lord always. I will say it again: Rejoice! Let your graciousness be known to everyone. The Lord is near. Don't worry about anything, but in everything, through prayer and petition with thanksgiving, present your requests to God. And the peace of God, which surpasses all understanding, will guard your hearts and minds in Christ Jesus.

PHILIPPIANS 4:4-7

But everything that was a gain to me, I have considered to be a loss because of Christ. More than that, I also consider everything to be a loss in view of the surpassing value of knowing Christ Jesus my Lord. Because of him I have suffered the loss of all things and consider them as dung, so that I may gain Christ and be found in him, not having a righteousness of my own from the law, but one that is through faith in Christ—the righteousness from God based on faith. My goal is to know him and the power of his resurrection and the fellowship of his sufferings, being conformed to his death, assuming that I will somehow reach the resurrection from among the dead.

○

PHILIPPIANS 3:7–11

Colossians & Philemon

Genre | **EPISTLE**

Since the fullness of God dwells in Jesus the Messiah, we should live out new-creation life accordingly rather than seeking wisdom, knowledge, or salvation in any kind of philosophy, rituals, or spiritual powers (Colossians). Followers of Jesus should regard one another's identity in the Messiah as more fundamental than our societal status and therefore treat one another with dignity, equality, and love (Philemon).

INTRODUCTION

AUTHOR The apostle Paul is identified as the author of Colossians (1:1; 4:18). The church fathers unreservedly endorsed Pauline authorship. Also favoring the authenticity of Colossians as a letter of Paul is its close connection with Philemon, an epistle widely regarded as Pauline.

BACKGROUND Paul wrote Colossians and Philemon during his first Roman imprisonment (Col 4:3,10,18; cp. Acts 28:30–31) in the early AD 60s. Together with Philemon, Philippians, and Ephesians, Colossians is commonly classified as a Prison Epistle. All four epistles share several personal links that warrant this conclusion (Eph 6:21–22; Col 1:7; 4:7–8,17; Phlm 2,12,23).

MESSAGE AND PURPOSE Paul wrote to counter the "Colossian heresy" that he considered an affront to the gospel of Jesus Christ. The false teaching is identified as a "philosophy" (Col 2:8), presumably drawn from some Hellenistic traditions as indicated by the references to "his fullness" (1:19), the "elements of this world" (Gk. *stoicheia*, 2:8,20), "wisdom" (2:3,23), and "self-made religion" (2:23). In addition, the false teaching contained Jewish elements such as circumcision (2:11; 3:11); "human tradition" (2:8), Sabbath observance, food regulations, festival participation (2:16); the "worship of angels" together with "access to a visionary realm" (2:18); and harsh human regulations (2:21–23). Paul addressed this syncretistic philosophy by setting forth a proper understanding of the gospel of Jesus Christ and by noting appropriate implications for Christian conduct. Although in Philemon, Paul addresses the letter to Apphia, Archippus, and the church that meets in Philemon's house (vv. 1–2), the main addressee is Philemon himself, for "you" or "your" (vv. 2,4–21,23) is singular and refers to Philemon. Apparently he was a prosperous businessman living in Colossae (implied in Col 4:9) whose household included several slaves and whose house was large enough to accommodate meetings of the young church.

SUMMARY Paul's letter to the church at Colossae is one of the Prison Epistles (along with Ephesians, Philippians, and Philemon). Paul's desire with this letter was to correct the false teachings that were cropping up in the church. In doing so, Paul presented a clear picture of Jesus Christ as supreme Lord of the universe, head of the church, and the only one through whom forgiveness is possible. Philemon is Paul's only letter of a private nature. It concerns a runaway slave, Onesimus, who had robbed his master, Philemon, and escaped from Colossae to Rome.

STRUCTURE Colossians may be divided into two main parts. The first (1:3–2:23) is a vigorous criticism of false teachings. The second (3:1–4:17) is made up of exhortations to proper Christian living. This is typical of Paul's approach, presenting a theology position first, a position on which the practical exhortations are built. The introduction (1:1–2) is in the form of a Hellenistic, personal letter. Notable in the final section are the mention of Onesimus (4:9), which links this letter with Philemon; the mention of a letter at Laodicea (4:16) that may have been Ephesians; and Paul's concluding signature, which indicates that the letter was prepared by an amanuensis (secretary; see 4:18).

Outlines

prōtotokos

Greek pronunciation:
[proh TAH tah kahs]

CSB translation:
firstborn

Uses in Colossians: 2
Uses in the NT: 8

Focus passage:
Colossians 1:15

Prōtotokos (*firstborn*) appears eight times in the NT. All six occurrences in the singular refer to Jesus, and it is possible that *prōtotokos* was a title for the incarnate Christ (Heb 1:6). In Luke 2:7 and Hebrews 11:28, *prōtotokos* clearly refers to *firstborn* children. But elsewhere in the NT, the term takes on the sense of "preeminence in rank or time." Jesus's preeminent status over his creation is seen in Colossians 1:15. As Creator "he is before all things" in supremacy (Col 1:17a) and is "the *firstborn* from the dead" (Col 1:18; Rev 1:5): the first to be resurrected and the one having authority over the resurrection of the dead. Additionally, Jesus's postresurrection transfiguration is a preview of the glorious transfiguration of the saints in the future (Rom 8:29).

klēronomia

Greek pronunciation:
[klay rah nah MEE ah]

CSB translation:
inheritance

Uses in Colossians: 1
Uses in the NT: 14

Focus passage:
Colossians 3:24

Klēronomia (*inheritance*) occasionally refers to promised possessions (Acts 7:5) or to the *inheritance* legally due an heir (Luke 12:13). More frequently, however, NT authors employ the term *inheritance* in a religious, spiritual sense to refer to the future, heavenly, imperishable, eternal salvation of which the saints will one day partake in the kingdom of God (Col 3:24; Eph 1:14; Heb 9:15; 1 Pet 1:4). Jesus, in his parable of the Vineyard Owner (Matt 21:38 = Mark 12:7 = Luke 20:14), loads the term with this deeper, spiritual referent, interpreting the *inheritance* as the kingdom of God (Matt 21:43). Paul speaks of *inheritance* only in this religious sense. Christians, as heirs of God through faith (Gal 3:26), have sole rights to this future *inheritance* (Eph 5:5). The sealing of the Holy Spirit upon believers is the Father's guarantee that he will grant his children their promised *inheritance* (Eph 1:13–14,18).

Ephesians and Colossians

EPHESIANS	COLOSSIANS	THEME
1:7	1:14–20	The Son's redemptive work
1:10	1:20	Everything comes together in Christ
1:15–17	1:3–4,9	Prayers for Paul's readers
1:18	1:27	Inheritance and hope for those in Christ's glory
1:21–22	1:16–18	Christ's authority over all
2:5	1:16–18	Believers are alive in Christ
2:12–13	1:21–22	Citizenship/redemption through Christ's blood
2:15	2:14	Abolished the law
3:1	4:3	Paul as a prisoner
3:2–3	1:25–26	Hidden mystery is made known
3:6–7	1:23–25	Paul, servant of the gospel
4:1	1:10	Live worthy of your calling
4:2	3:12–13	Humility, gentleness, patience, bearing with one another in love
4:15–16	2:19	Christ is the head of the body
4:22–23	3:5–12	Put off the old nature and put on the new
5:3–6	3:5–9	No immorality, impurity, or greed
5:15	4:5	Live wisely
5:19–20	3:16–17	Sing and give thanks to God
5:21–6:9	3:18–4:1	Specific instructions for wives, husbands, children, parents, slaves, and masters
6:18–20	4:2–3	Perseverance in prayer
6:21–22	4:7–8	Tychicus sent to give updates on Paul and encourage the churches

What Gnostics Believe

Gnosticism is difficult to define because the term is used for a collection of divergent movements. It is derived from the Greek word for knowledge (*gnosis*). Usually Gnosticism refers to a second-century Christian heresy that was a major threat to the church. The main ideas in gnostic systems include the following:

1. A dualism exists in the universe between God and a lesser, evil being usually called the Demiurge.

2. God is unknowable. He has no concern for the world and nothing to do with it.

3. Various beings emerge from God and join in male and female pairs to form concentric barriers around God.

4. The female being in the last barrier, without her male partner, gave birth to the Demiurge.

5. The Demiurge created the world, and therefore anything material (including the body) is evil.

6. A spark of the divine was also placed in humans (or at least some of them) that needs to be awakened and called back to the divine.

7. A revealer calls humans and shows the way through the barriers. Christ was viewed as the revealer, but he was not truly human. He only took over Jesus's body at his baptism and left before his death.

8. Knowledge of one's true self and of the character of the universe is the way to salvation. Salvation is achieved when at death or at the end of the world a person passes through the barriers and is reintegrated into God.

ORIGINS OF GNOSTICISM

Little is known about the origins of Gnosticism. It had no one founder, even though the name Simon Magus (see Acts 8) was often associated in church traditions with the rise of Gnosticism. Gnosticism had no founding text, nor can a specific time of beginning for the movement be identified. Some of the ideas in Gnosticism were already current in the New Testament times. But although debated, there is no evidence that Gnosticism existed before Christianity. Some facts about the origins of Gnosticism are clear. This religion arose because of a deeply felt spiritual need. One of the main concerns was the problem of evil. The gnostic understanding of the universe was a way to protect God from any responsibility for the evil in this world. Ideas were gathered from various religions, especially Judaism. The focus on knowledge and light is present in nearly every religion. An awareness of Gnosticism reminds us that knowledge does not save; a faith relationship with Christ does.

Slavery in the First Century

Slavery, the legal possession of an individual by another, was the primary "energy source" for the Greco-Roman world. Slaves were employed in agricultural and manufacturing enterprises, construction, mining, governmental positions, education of children, cultural and entertainment activities, and many routine household duties.

In the Roman Empire slavery was unrelated to race. Most scholars believe it began as generals chose to enslave conquered enemies rather than execute them. Slavery was also a form of punishment for crimes or a means of dealing with debtors unable to repay loans.

By the first century there were thousands of slaves in all parts of the empire. By the time Augustus became the Roman emperor in AD 63, there were some 3 million slaves (400,000 in the city of Rome) within a total population of 7.5 million Romans.

A slave's status and treatment differed greatly. Slaves were not completely without legal rights. They were free from taxation and military service, had the right to common-law marriage, and could join social groups or associations.

Kind and considerate treatment was extended—if not on humanitarian grounds, then because it was prudent to care for one's "property." Slaves were valuable property. In New Testament times the price of a slave was about nine times the wages paid a laborer for a year. A slave could be sold privately or at public auction at the will of the owner.

The New Testament attests that slaves were members of the early church. Both Christian slaves and masters are told their relationship must be controlled by their common relationship in Christ. Philemon was enjoined to receive the runaway slave Onesimus as "a faithful and dearly loved brother" (Col 4:9), thus elevating the nonperson to the status of an equal. Slavery furnishes New Testament imagery for the status of the sinner under sin and of the Christian to God. In his incarnation Christ accepted the role of slave (or "servant," Phil 2:7). Terms such as "ransom" and "redeem" reminded New Testament readers of the parallels between the purchase of their spiritual freedom and that of the physical freedom of the slave.

Seven Observations about Slavery and the New Testament

In their book *The New Testament in Its World,* biblical scholars N. T. Wright and Michael F. Bird offer the following seven observations about slavery in the first-century world in which the apostle Paul ministered. Below is a summary of these observations:

1) **To ancient people, slavery seemed like a "fact of life," like it or not.** Slavery was deeply embedded within the social structure, welfare system, and economic activity of the ancient world; no one living at the time could have fathomed how society could work without the institution of slavery. Some discussed the treatment of slaves in philosophical contexts, but the convention of slavery was accepted as a given necessity, not something open to debate.

2) **No civil process or revolutionary movement could have realistically brought about the end of slavery in the ancient world.** In the absence of modern-day political structures, such as representative democracy and libertarian ethics, no effective method existed for abolishing the slave trade in a widespread, revolutionary way.

3) **The quality of a slave's life depended mostly upon the slave's master.** This meant the most realistic and effective way to improve the life of a slave was for a master to treat him or her with kindness and justice, perhaps extending manumission at some point—or to be kept under the care of a master but as a free person (see Eph 6:9 ; Col 4:1; Phlm 8–17).

4) **Freedom was sometimes a possibility for slaves.** Hence, Paul exhorted slaves who were Christians to pursue their freedom if it was obtainable (1 Cor 7:20–22).

5) **The New Testament does not endorse or sanitize slavery.** In fact, Paul casted slavery in a negative moral light by listing "slave traders" in 1 Timothy 1:9–10 among other sinful behaviors.

6) **The New Testament affirms the equality of slaves with all other people and promotes a matching social ethic within the church.** Paul, for instance, stated that for those in Christ there are no ethnic or socioeconomic distinctions that make someone any more or less valuable: "There is no Jew or Greek, slave or free, male and female; since you are all one in Christ Jesus" (Gal 3:28). In other words, slaves and masters are regarded as equal in the kingdom of God (see also 1 Cor 12:13; Col 3:11; cp. Eph 6:8).

7) **The case of Philemon and Onesimus illustrates the radical effect the gospel should have on the slave-master relationship.** Paul instructed Philemon as a slave owner in good standing within the church to receive Onesimus "no longer as a slave, but more than a slave—as a dearly loved brother" (Phlm 16). This sort of dynamic was a drastic departure from the norm at the time and certainly would not have been characteristic of how a master would respond to a slave who had run away. Hence, in Paul's encouragement in the letter, we see an ethic that would sow the seeds of slavery's eventual downfall.

Key Takeaway: "In sum, Paul was certainly no William Wilberforce; but without Paul, the ethic that drove William Wilberforce and his friends might not have existed."[6]

1-2 Thessalonians

Genre | **EPISTLE**

Because of Jesus's promised return, Christians can endure persecution and suffering while pursuing a godly life, knowing that God has chosen them for salvation and sanctification (1 Thessalonians). Amid persecution and affliction, Christians can stand firm in the gospel knowing that Jesus will return to vindicate his people and judge the unbelieving world (2 Thessalonians).

INTRODUCTION

AUTHOR

No serious objections have been made to dispute that Paul was the author of 1 Thessalonians (1:1). The greeting also mentions Silvanus and Timothy. Sometimes Paul wrote from the team perspective, but he was the primary author (2:18; 3:2).

BACKGROUND

Thessalonica was a large port city on the Aegean Sea in modern-day Greece, with a population of about two hundred thousand. The city was filled with pagan worshipers of idols, the full pantheon of Greek and Roman gods, and was well known for its emperor worship. Thessalonica was loyal to Caesar, who had granted its citizens many privileges.

MESSAGE AND PURPOSE

Timothy reported to Paul that although the church at Thessalonica was suffering affliction, they were holding fast to the faith. And though they had some doctrinal misunderstandings, they were laboring for the Lord out of love and patiently hoping for the return of Christ. In 1 Thessalonians, Paul wrote to encourage the church in their faith, to remind them that sanctification was God's will for them, and to correct misunderstandings about end-time events. In 2 Thessalonians, Paul assured them that the day of the Lord had not yet come since certain end-time events had not yet taken place and the "lawless one" was currently restrained from appearing (2:6–8). This appears to be the primary impetus for the letter. The fact that some people in the Thessalonian church had stopped working may suggest that their incorrect view was leading to laziness and irresponsibility (3:10–11).

SUMMARY

Paul spent a very short time in the city of Thessalonica, but he was able to establish a church during his stay. He may have had little time to instruct the new converts, so it is not surprising that Paul wrote a letter to address some questions (1 Thessalonians). Following up on his first letter to the Thessalonians, Paul wrote to give further clarification on how to live the Christian life in light of the return of Christ. The Thessalonians were called to stand firm and live useful lives because the return of Christ might be in the distant future (2 Thessalonians).

STRUCTURE

The body of 1 Thessalonians does not follow Paul's typical structure of presenting doctrine first, followed by practical exhortation based on that doctrine. Instead, the letter moves back and forth between the doctrinal and the practical. The tone of Paul's second letter to the Thessalonians is markedly "cooler" than his first letter. In this second letter, though, Paul expressed grave concern about the spiritual state of the Thessalonian believers and gave them a sharp rebuke about congregational life (3:6–15). His style is typical of his other letters—a doctrinal section followed by practical exhortation.

Outlines

WORD STUDY

stephanos

Greek pronunciation:
[STEH fah nahs]

CSB translation:
crown

Uses in 1 Thessalonians: 1
Uses in the NT: 18

Focus passage:
1 Thessalonians 2:19

In the Gospels, *stephanos* (*crown*) refers exclusively to the thorny *crown* Jesus wore during his passion (Matt 27:29; Mark 15:17; John 19:2,5). Paul consistently exhorts the saints by using the promise of a *crown* as their future reward. Believers should run the Christian race to obtain an imperishable *crown*, even as athletes run for a perishable *crown* (1 Cor 9:25; cp. Rev 3:11) and a *crown* of righteousness belongs to all who love the Lord's appearing (2 Tim 4:8). Certain congregations are the *crown* with which Paul will appear before the Lord at his return (Phil 4:1; 1 Thess 2:19). James speaks of a *crown* of life given to those who, despite persecution, maintain their love for God (Jas 1:12; cp. Rev 2:10), and an unfading *crown* of glory awaits elders who lovingly shepherd their congregations (1 Pet 5:4). *Crown* appears frequently in the apocalyptic imagery of Revelation. There it is usually associated with pictures of authority, rule, dominion, power, and/or enablement for a task. Another Greek word for *crown* (*diadēma*) occurs three times in the NT (Rev 12:3; 13:1; 19:12).

harpazō

Greek pronunciation:
[hahr PAH zoh]

CSB translation:
caught up

Uses in 1 Thessalonians: 1
Uses in the NT: 14

Focus passage:
1 Thessalonians 4:17

Harpazō (*catch up, snatch up*) is often invested with the idea of force. In this sense, *harpazō* refers to a rescue (*take away*, Acts 23:10) and to the near-forceful capture of Jesus by a crowd (John 6:15). The term is not limited to the physical realm. The evil one *snatches away* the message of the kingdom sown upon men's hearts (Matt 13:19), Jude exhorts believers to *snatch* some men from the fire (Jude 23), and no one is able to *snatch* the sheep belonging to the good shepherd from our Father's hand (John 10:11,28–29). Elsewhere, the term is used of supernatural phenomena and does not carry the concept of force. Paul received glorious revelation after being *caught up* into paradise (2 Cor 12:2,4). The Holy Spirit *carries* Philip *away* and transports him to Azotus (Acts 8:39). Believers will one day be *caught up* to meet their returning Lord (1 Thess 4:17).

parousia

Greek pronunciation:
[pah roo SEE ah]

CSB translation:
coming

Uses in 2 Thessalonians: 3
Uses in the NT: 24

Focus passage:
2 Thessalonians 2:8

Parousia means *presence* or *coming*. In the sense of *presence*, it refers to physical proximity. Paul speaks of the obedience of the Philippian church during both his *presence* and his absence (Phil 2:12) and of the *presence* of his fellow laborers (1 Cor 16:17). Elsewhere, *parousia* refers to the *coming* or *arrival* of men or events. Paul mentions the *arrival* of Titus (2 Cor 7:6–7), and he hopes to *come* again to the Philippians (Phil 1:26). *Parousia* occurs most often in relation to the *coming* of the Lord Jesus as human history moves to closure. His *coming* will be preceded by the *coming* of the "lawless one," the antichrist (2 Thess 2:8–9). The glorious *coming* of Jesus will be accompanied by the destruction of all his enemies, a resurrection of the dead in Christ, and a gathering of the saints still living (1 Cor 15:23–25; 1 Thess 4:15–16; 2 Thess 2:1).

1–2 Thessalonians Timeline

2300–150 BC

2300
Prehistoric settlement on the site of Thessalonica

600
Founding of Therme at the head of the Thermaic Gulf

316
Cassander, king of Macedon, establishes Thessalonica at the site where Therme had existed, naming the new city in honor of his wife.

168
The Romans gain control of Thessalonica when Perseus, king of Macedonia, is defeated at Pydna.

168–103
First Jewish community in Thessalonica, emigrants from Alexandria

149–42 BC

147–120
Construction of the Macedonian leg of the Egnatian Way, a Roman military road connecting Thessalonica with the Adriatic Sea in the west and with Neapolis in the east

146
Thessalonica becomes the capital of the Roman province of Macedonia and is referred to as "the Mother of Macedonia."

58
The Roman statesman Cicero spends six months of his self-imposed exile in Thessalonica.

49–48
Many Roman officials flee Rome and take up residence in Thessalonica during the Roman civil war.

42
Augustus declares Thessalonica a free city following the battle of Philippi.

AD 33–56

33
Jesus's trials, death, resurrection, and ascension

44
Claudius Caesar restores Thessalonica's status as a free city.

50
Paul, Silas, and Timothy preach in Thessalonica.

51
Paul writes 1 Thessalonians.

51
Paul writes a second letter to the Thessalonian believers.

52
Paul concludes his second missionary journey and arrives in Antioch of Syria.

56
Paul likely revisits the Thessalonian Christians as he visits the churches planted in Macedonia.

The Man of Lawlessness

"The man of lawlessness" in 2 Thessalonians 2:3 (CSB) is also called "the man of sin" (KJV). The two words are sometimes used interchangeably; therefore, either would describe an evil man. "It is not a personal name but a characterization of the man, indicating his evil character." [7]

HIS ACTIONS

"This man will oppose everything connected with the divine—not only Christianity but anything that has to do with theism. This man will wage war against everything that hints at religion, faith, or spirituality." [8] At the same time, he exalts himself as though he were God. In order to support his claims to deity, he performs "every kind of miracle, both signs and wonders" (2 Thess 2:9). Paul implies that many of the miracles will be deceptions, not miracles at all. Others, though, will be real, done through the power of Satan, not Christ. The man of lawlessness is a false Christ. He is a person, not just an influence. He is not Satan, but he is used by Satan.

HIS TIME

In 2 Thessalonians 2:1–3, Paul told them two things that would precede the day of the Lord. One was "the apostasy," and the other was the coming of the man of lawlessness.

Paul said, "The mystery of lawlessness is already at work" (2 Thess 2:7). This is like John's claim that many antichrists were already at work (1 John 2:18). Throughout history there have been evil people who had more than one of the characteristics of the man of lawlessness. But none of them has been the biblical antichrist. The one ultimate son of perdition will come in the final days. We do not know when that will be, but we can stand for Christ and oppose evil in our own time—leaving the actual time of the revelation of the man of lawlessness in God's hands.

HIS DESTINY

The appearance and actions of the man of lawlessness are frightening to consider, but we must not forget that God is sovereign. God's victory over evil is evident throughout the Word of God.

Paul's purpose in dealing with issues related to the day of the Lord was not just to satisfy people's curiosity. Instead, he wrote to warn them against being deceived and to encourage them to remain faithful to Christ to the end.

The Return of Christ

The Lord Jesus, who was raised from the dead and ascended to the Father, will return. This conviction is expressed repeatedly in the New Testament.

The church used several terms to refer to the return of Christ. *Parousia*, meaning either *coming* or *presence*, often described the Lord's return (see Matt 24:3; 1 Cor 15:23; 1 Thess 2:19). *Epiphaneia* in religious usage described the *appearing* of an unseen god (see Titus 2:13). The revelation (*apocalypsis*) of the power and glory of the Lord was eagerly anticipated by the church (for example, see Luke 17:30; Rom 8:18).

The phrase "the day of the Lord" (an OT theme) is also common in the New Testament. "That day," "the day of Christ," and similar phrases were used as synonyms.

Often the writer implied that he was living in the last days (Acts 2:17; 1 John 2:18). The reference to time in many passages listed above, however, is ambiguous (see 1 Cor 1:8; 5:5; Phil 1:6,10; 1 Thess 5:2; 2 Thess 1:10). The character of that "day" is clearer than its timing. It is a day of judgment.

THE GOSPELS

Jesus taught his disciples to expect a catastrophic conclusion to history. At that time God would effect a general resurrection and a final judgment with appropriate rewards for the just and the unjust (Matt 7:21–27; 24:1–51; Mark 12:24–27; 13:1–37; Luke 11:31–32; 21:5–36).

Although the signs of the end receive considerable attention in the Gospels (Matt 24; Mark 13; Luke 21), the time of the end remains obscure. Some sayings imply the end is near (Matt 10:23; Mark 9:1; 13:30). Others imply a delay (Matt 25:5; Mark 13:7,10). The clearest statements indicate that the time cannot be known (Matt 24:36,42,44; Mark 13:32–37; Luke 12:35–40).

Acts 1:6–8 expresses the same conviction: the time cannot be known. According to Jesus, the disciple's task was to bear witness to the gospel. The time was left in the Father's hands.

THE EPISTLES

As the church aged, questions arose. What happens to those who die before Jesus's return (1 Thess 4:13–18)? What will his return be like, and when will it occur (1 Thess 5:1–11; 2 Thess 2:1–12)? What will happen to us and our world (1 Cor 15:12–13,23–28)? Does his delay make his promised return a lie (2 Pet 3:3–10)?

The New Testament answers these questions with a strong affirmation concerning Christ's return. The New Testament is not as clear regarding the time of his appearing. Yet the Epistles clearly reveal a persistent faith in the return of Christ (Rom 8:19–39; 2 Tim 4:1). His lordship is real. His victory is assured. His people will share his glory at his return (Rev 19:6–22:17). Thus the responsibility of the church is patience, faithfulness, and witness (see Acts 1:7–8; 1 Cor 15:58; 1 Thess 4:18).

The Day of the Lord

The day of the Lord marks the point when God reveals his sovereignty over human powers and human existence. The day of the Lord rests on the Hebrew term *yom*, "day," the fifth most frequent noun used in the Old Testament and one used with a variety of meanings: the time of daylight from sunrise to sunset (Gen 1:14; 3:8; 8:22; Amos 5:8), a 24-hour period (Gen 1:5), a general expression for "time" without specific limits (Gen 2:4; Ps 102:3; Isa 7:17), the period of a specific event (Jer 32:31; Ezek 1:28). "Day of the Lord" then does not give a precise time period. It may mean the daylight hours, the 24-hour day, or a general time period, perhaps characterized by a special event. Zechariah 14:7 even points to a time when all time is daylight, night with its darkness having vanished.

"Day of the Lord" does not in itself designate the time perspective of the event, whether it is past, present, or future. Lamentations 2:1 can speak of the "day of his anger" in past tense, describing the fall of Jerusalem. Joel 1:15 could describe a present disaster as the "day of the Lord."

The Old Testament prophets used a term familiar to their audience, a term by which the audience expected light and salvation (Amos 5:18), but the prophets painted it as a day of darkness and judgment (Isa 2:10–22; 13:6,9; Joel 1:15; 2:1–11,31; 3:14–15; Amos 5:20; Zeph 1:7–8,14–18; Mal 4:5). The Old Testament language of the day of the Lord is thus aimed at warning sinners among God's people of the danger of trusting in traditional religion without commitment to God and his way of life. It is language that could be aimed at judging Israel or that could be used to promise deliverance from evil enemies (Isa 13:6,9; Ezek 30:3; Obad 15). The day of the Lord is thus a point in time in which God displays his sovereign initiative to reveal his control of history, of time, of his people, and of all people.

New Testament writers took up the Old Testament expression to point to Christ's final victory and the final judgment of sinners. In so doing, they used several different expressions: "day of Christ Jesus" (Phil 1:6), "day of our Lord Jesus Christ" (1 Cor 1:8), "day of the Lord" (1 Cor 5:5; 1 Thess 5:2), "day of Christ" (Phil 1:10; 2:16), "day of judgment" (1 John 4:17), "this day" (1 Thess 5:4), "that day" (2 Tim 1:12), "day of wrath" (Rom 2:5).

The day of the Lord points to the promise that God's eternal sovereignty over all creation and all nations will one day become crystal clear to all creatures.

1–2 Timothy & Titus

Genre | **EPISTLE**

Generational faithfulness to the gospel entails the promotion of sound teaching and the installing of stable leadership structures within the local church, both of which are conducive to godly living among Christians (1 Timothy). Having received the apostolic deposit and commission, Christian pastors and leaders should live unashamed of the gospel through the power of the Holy Spirit in holding on to the pattern of sound teaching that is in accord with sacred Scripture (2 Timothy). Within the local church, qualified leaders and sound doctrine are vital for gospel ministry and ongoing Christian formation unto good works (Titus).

INTRODUCTION

AUTHOR As stated in the opening of each letter, these letters were written by Paul (1 Tim 1:1; 2 Tim 1:1; Titus 1:1). However, many scholars today assume that Paul did not write them. This opinion is based on the differences from his other letters in vocabulary and style, alleged differences in theology, and uncertainties about where these letters fit chronologically in the life of the apostle. But the differences in style and vocabulary are not troublesome when one considers that authors often use different vocabulary when addressing different groups and situations. In spite of significant opposition by some scholars, there is a solid basis for accepting the Pastoral Epistles as Pauline.

BACKGROUND Paul most likely wrote these letters after the time covered in the book of Acts. After being released from prison, as is traditionally supposed, he visited Crete and other places. First Timothy and Titus were written during this period of further mission work. Eventually Paul was imprisoned again, and this led to his execution. During this final imprisonment, Paul wrote 2 Timothy as he anticipated his martyrdom.

MESSAGE AND PURPOSE In each of these letters, Paul instructed one of his younger coworkers in living out his faith and teaching others to do the same. Each letter is concerned significantly with false teaching and its harmful effects in the church. In each letter Paul wrote to affirm his representative before the church, to hold up the standard of right doctrine, and to show that right doctrine must result in proper living.

SUMMARY First Timothy, 2 Timothy, and Titus have been referred to as the Pastoral Epistles since the eighteenth century. It is reasonable to consider these letters together since they have striking similarities in style, vocabulary, and setting. These letters stand apart from the other Pauline letters because they were the only ones written to Paul's gospel coworkers. They were written primarily not to describe church structure or pastoral ministry (contrary to popular opinion) but to teach Christian living in response to the gospel.

STRUCTURE All three letters follow the typical pattern of a Greek epistle. While there are some lexical differences with many of Paul's other letters, keep in mind that these letters were written to specific individuals. One thing unique to the structure of these letters is the focus on church leadership.

Outlines

diakonos

Greek Pronunciation:
[dee AH kah nahs]

CSB translation:
deacon, servant

Uses in 1 Timothy: 3
Uses in the NT: 29

Focus passage:
1 Timothy 3:8,12

Diakonos frequently refers to a *servant* who attends to others' needs. Those responsible for serving a meal (John 2:5,9) and the *attendants* of a king are *servants* (Matt 22:13). The person desiring a position of greatness must become a *servant* (Mark 10:43). One can also serve a spiritual power. False apostles are called *servants* of Satan (2 Cor 11:15), and Paul is a *servant* of the gospel (Eph 3:7). Governing authorities are *servants* of God, for they dispense justice (Rom 13:4). Elsewhere, *diakonos* retains the idea of *service*, while adopting the more technical sense of a church leadership position (i.e., *deacon*). Paul may use this technical sense when he calls Phoebe a *servant* of the church in Cenchreae (Rom 16:1). In 1 Timothy 3:8–13, Paul delineates the qualifications for assuming this church position.

sōtēr

Greek Pronunciation:
[soh TAYR]

CSB translation:
Savior

Uses in 1 Timothy: 3
Uses in the NT: 24

Focus passage:
1 Timothy 4:10

Outside the NT, the title *sōtēr* (*savior, deliverer*) was applied to deserving men, leading officials, rulers, or deities (e.g., Roman emperors Julius Caesar, Nero, and Vespasian). The term had connotations of *protector, deliverer, preserver,* or *savior*. In the NT, *sōtēr* refers exclusively to Jesus Christ and to God the Father, with a focus on their *saving,* delivering character as expressed through their actions. As *Savior,* Christ grants repentance and forgiveness of sin (Acts 5:31), *protects* and *saves* the church (Eph 5:23), will come again to deliver his people from this world (Phil 3:20), has made possible the outpouring of the Spirit (Titus 3:6), has abolished death (2 Tim 1:10), and has authority in his kingdom (2 Pet 1:11). God is "the *Savior* of all people, especially of those who believe" (1 Tim 4:10), and "wants everyone to be *saved*" (1 Tim 2:4). He manifested his love in his *saving* acts toward the church (Titus 3:4), he poured out the Holy Spirit (Titus 3:6), and he deserves praise and adoration (Jude 25).

aphtharsia

Greek pronunciation:
[ahf thahr SEE ah]

CSB translation:
immortality

Uses in 2 Timothy: 1
Uses in the NT: 7

Focus passage:
2 Timothy 1:10

The apostle Paul uses *aphtharsia* (*incorruption, immortality*) in reference to two concepts: physical state and temporal aspect. With respect to physical state, *aphtharsia* refers to the state of not being subject to perishing or decay (i.e., *incorruption*). For example, in 1 Corinthians 15, Paul uses *aphtharsia* four times to refer to the resurrection body. So, the Christian's corruptible, earthly body will be changed to *incorruption* (i.e., the state of being imperishable) through resurrection from the dead (1 Cor 15:42,50,53–54). Naturally, that which is *incorruptible* is also *immortal*. The relationship of these two concepts provides the bridge to the temporal aspect of *aphtharsia,* in which the term refers to a continuous state or process (*immortality*). Christ Jesus abolished death and brought life and *immortality* (i.e., continuous life) to light through the gospel (2 Tim 1:10).

1–2 Timothy & Titus Timeline

AD 5–50

5
Paul is born in Tarsus of Cilicia.

34
Paul's conversion to Christ as he travels to Damascus

49
Paul takes Titus and Barnabas from Antioch to Jerusalem for the Jerusalem Council.

50
Paul and Silas return to Lystra and take Timothy with them as they travel through Asia Minor to Troas.

50
Timothy ministers with Paul and Silas in Philippi, Thessalonica, and Berea.

AD 51–56

51
Paul has to flee to Athens; he leaves Timothy and Silas to continue the work in Berea.

51
Timothy rejoins Paul in Athens and brings word of the work in Macedonia.

51–52
Timothy returns to Thessalonica to encourage the new believers.

52
Timothy joins Paul in his ministry in Corinth, bringing word of progress in Thessalonica.

54–56
Timothy comes to Ephesus to work with Paul during Paul's three-year ministry.

AD 56–62

56
Paul sends Timothy with the 1 Corinthians letter to the troubled church in Corinth.

56
While ministering in Ephesus, Paul sends Titus to mediate the conflict between Paul and the church at Corinth.

57
Paul comes to Corinth in person, and from there he writes the letter to the Romans.

62
Upon his release from his first imprisonment, Paul goes to Ephesus and appoints Timothy as chief pastor.

AD 62–67

62–64
Paul writes 1 Timothy and Titus.

62–64
Paul commissions Titus to train leaders for the young Christian congregations on Crete.

JULY 18–24, 64
Major persecution of the Christians in Rome begins following the great fire.

64–67?
Paul returns to Rome, is arrested, and writes 2 Timothy from the Mamertine Prison.

67?
Paul's martyrdom in Rome.

Paul's Voyage to Rome

City

PAUL'S PATH TO ROME

ETESIAN WINDS

Ship smashes into reef and all aboard swim to shore

Ship lost in storm

Paul spends two years preaching the gospel as he awaits his appeal to Nero.

Destination of Paul's letters to Titus

Destination of Paul's letters to Timothy

Change to a larger grain ship

Porcius Festus sends Paul to Rome to appeal to Caesar.

MEDITERRANEAN SEA

TYRRHENIAN SEA

ADRIATIC SEA

Sicily

ITALIA

Puteoli

Pompeii

Rhegium

Crete

Lasea

Ephesus

ASIA

PHRYGIA

LYCIA

Myra

PAMPHYLIA

Cyprus

CILICIA

SYRIA

Sidon

Jerusalem

DEAD SEA

EGYPT

BLACK SEA

Rh

N
S
E
W

0
100
200
300 Kilometers

0
100
200
300 Miles

Models of Church Structure

Paul appointed leaders wherever he planted churches. Sometimes these leaders carried unofficial designations, such as "those who labor among you and lead you in the Lord" (1 Thess 5:12). At other times they had official titles such as "elder" (*presbyteros*, Titus 1:5), "overseer" or bishop (*episkopos*, Titus 1:7), or "deacon" (*diakonos*, 1 Tim 3:8). In the New Testament the terms *elder* and *bishop* are interchangeable and describe the same function. The qualifications for each are the same (1 Tim 3:1–7; Titus 1:5–9). Within church leadership models, these are the most common roles:

DEACONS

In the New Testament the noun refers to ministers of the gospel (Col 1:23), ministers of Christ, servants of God, those who follow Jesus, and other similar roles. By the second century, deacons filled an important role in the ministry of the early church, serving the needs of the poor, assisting in baptism and the Lord's Supper, and performing other practical ministerial tasks.

ELDERS/BISHOPS

Although there are a few specific details about the function of elders in the Jerusalem church, they apparently served as a decision-making council. However, elders in the Pauline churches were probably spiritual leaders and ministers, not simply a governing council (Rom 12:6–9). Some scholars believe bishops and elders are interchangeable.

PASTORS

The background of the term lies in the biblical image of the people of God as God's flock (Jer 23:1–4; Ezek 34:1–16; Luke 12:32; John 10:16). Pastoral ministry is closely associated with teaching (Eph 4:11) as God's gift to the church. Such ministry fulfills its God-ordained purpose when it trains church members to be mature in faith and equipped for ministry, unifying the church in Christian faith and knowledge (Eph 4:12–13).

Timothy's Ministry Assignments

DURING PAUL'S SECOND MISSIONARY JOURNEY

ASSIGNMENT IN THESSALONICA

- Paul sent Timothy back to Thessalonica from Athens because of Paul's concern for the church (1 Thess 3:1–2).
- Paul sent Timothy to encourage the Thessalonian Christians and then report back to him about the condition of the church.

ASSIGNMENT IN CORINTH

- Timothy rejoined Paul in Corinth and delivered the good report concerning the Thessalonian church (1 Thess 3:6–8).
- Paul commended the church for having stood strong in the face of opposition (1 Thess 1:6–10).
- Paul, Silas, and Timothy spent 18 months in Corinth, preaching and teaching about Jesus (Acts 18:11).

DURING PAUL'S THIRD MISSIONARY JOURNEY

RETURNING TO CORINTH

- Paul received word of problems in Corinth and sent Timothy back to a church where sin had become prominent, and the membership was challenging Paul's authority.
- Even though the Scriptures do not state definitively that Timothy failed, some have concluded he did and that Paul replaced Timothy with Titus.
- Timothy rejoined Paul in Macedonia and accompanied him throughout the remainder of the third missionary journey.

AFTER PAUL'S MISSIONARY JOURNEY

ASSIGNMENT IN EPHESUS

- While in Ephesus, Timothy received the epistles bearing his name—1 and 2 Timothy.
- Timothy was in Ephesus as Paul's representative to oppose false teachings and to instruct the Ephesian Christians about how they should conduct themselves.

Hebrews

Genre | **EPISTLE**

Jesus is the supreme revelation of God
and his purposes, having sat down in heaven as
our great high priest after obtaining salvation for his
people as the perfect mediator of the new covenant.

INTRODUCTION

AUTHOR The text of Hebrews does not identify its author. What we do know is that the author was a second-generation Christian, for he said he received the confirmed message of Christ from "those who heard" Jesus himself (2:3). Scholars have proposed the following persons as authors: Luke, Clement of Rome, Barnabas, Apollos, Timothy, Philip, Silas, Jude, and Aristion. Ultimately it does not matter that the identity of the author is now lost. We should be satisfied with the fact that early Christians received the letter as inspired and authoritative Scripture and that its value for Christian discipleship is unquestioned.

BACKGROUND The author of Hebrews knew his recipients well since he called them "brothers and sisters" (3:12; 7:5; 10:19; 13:22) and "dearly loved friends" (6:9). Like the writer, they were converts who had heard the gospel through the earliest followers of Christ (2:3). Regarding when the book was written, it is clear that the fall of Jerusalem (AD 70) had not yet occurred. The destruction of the temple would have been mentioned if it had already occurred, for it would have strengthened the letter's argument about Christ's sacrifice spelling the end of the temple sacrificial system.

MESSAGE AND PURPOSE The author of Hebrews wanted to exalt Jesus Christ. A verbal indication of this desire is the consistent and repetitive use of the Greek word *kreitton*, which means "more excellent," "superior," or "better." This word is the common thread that binds together the complex and subtle theological argumentation of the book. In comparison to everything else in the divine plan for creation and redemption, Jesus Christ is superior.

SUMMARY The Epistle to the Hebrews is a tribute to the incomparable Son of God and an encouragement to the author's persecuted fellow believers. The author feared that his Christian readers were wavering in their endurance. The writer had a twofold approach: (1) He exalted Jesus Christ, who is addressed as both "God" and "the son of man" (2:6), and is thus the only one who can serve as mediator between God and humanity. (2) He exhorted his fellow Christians to "go on to maturity" (6:1) and live by faith (11:1).

STRUCTURE If the literary style of Hebrews indicates anything, it is that it is a written theological sermon. It is not so much a letter—although it certainly ends like one—because it has no opening subscription, as was the norm with ancient letters. The sustained development of a complex, holistic theology of covenant indicates that Hebrews is a written theological sermon that discloses the broad sweep of God's grand redemptive plan for humanity.

Outline

WORD STUDY

katapausis

Greek pronunciation:
[kah TAH pow sis]

CSB translation:
rest

Uses in Hebrews: 8
Uses in the NT: 9

Focus passage:
Hebrews 4:1,3,5,10–11

In the NT, *katapausis* (*rest*) has multiple referents. Luke makes reference to a temple for God, the place where he would *rest* and live (Acts 7:49). Hebrews refers to *rest* as the Christian's future destination, the place of God's blessing. That *rest* is available to every generation of saints, but its realization comes only through obedience (Heb 4:2,6,11). God's *rest* at creation (4:4) points past Joshua and David (4:7–8) to this final *rest* for believers (4:9). For Moses and his generation, that *rest* was the promised land, the place of God's blessing (3:11,16–19). Unfortunately, that generation missed it (3:19). For Christians, *rest* is the final place of God's heavenly blessing, which they will receive if they hold fast their faith (4:11). The author of Hebrews strongly exhorts his audience to strive in obedience and perseverance to ensure they attain that future *rest* (4:1,11).

archiereus

Greek pronunciation:
[ahr kee eh ROOS]

CSB translation:
high priest

Uses in Hebrews: 17
Uses in the NT: 122

Focus passage:
Hebrews 5:10

In the Gospels and Acts, *archiereus* refers to the Jewish *high priest*, who served as president of the Sanhedrin, the Jewish supreme court (Matt 26:3,57; Acts 24:1). The plural (*chief priests*) indicates members of the priestly aristocracy from which the *high priest* was chosen. These *priests* were key figures in the Sanhedrin and belonged to the Sadducean party (Mark 14:55; Acts 5:17). In Hebrews, *archiereus* refers primarily to Christ's priestly ministry, which came from God (Heb 5:5,10) and was superior to that of any earthly *priest* (7:27–28). Christ is *high priest* of the new covenant, having accomplished the ultimate sacrifice (8:1–6). He passed through the heavens, entered the true sanctuary, offered himself as the one final sacrifice, and sat down at God's right hand (4:14; 6:20; 7:27; 8:1–2; 9:12). Jesus is able to deal mercifully with his people because he was fully human (2:17; 4:15; 5:1–10).

diathēkē

Greek pronunciation:
[dee ah THAY kay]

CSB translation:
covenant

Uses in Hebrews: 17
Uses in the NT: 33

Focus passage:
Hebrews 9:4

A *covenant* (*diathēkē*) is a legal arrangement between two parties (Gal 3:15) or a document, a *will*, transferring property from the deceased to an heir (Heb 9:16). The Greek OT influenced the use of *diathēkē* in the NT, where the *covenant* was an agreement by which God's people related to him. The NT frequently mentions three OT *covenants*: (1) the Abrahamic *covenant* (Gen 12:1–3; 15:1–21; 17:1–27), (2) the Mosaic *covenant* (Exod 20:1–24:8), and (3) the new *covenant* (Jer 31:31–34). The NT often focuses on the relationship between the Mosaic and new *covenants* (e.g., 2 Cor 3:6,14). Over half the occurrences of *diathēkē* in the NT occur in Hebrews, where Jesus is portrayed as mediator of the new *covenant*, a *covenant* superior to the Mosaic *covenant* (Heb 7:22; 8:6,8–10; 9:15). As the Mosaic *covenant* was inaugurated with blood, so the new *covenant* was inaugurated with Jesus's blood (10:18–28; 13:20; cp. Matt 26:28; 1 Cor 11:25).

HEBREWS

Titles of Jesus in Hebrews

APOSTLE AND HIGH PRIEST OF OUR CONFESSION

God's representative to humanity

Hebrews 3:1

PIONEER AND PERFECTER OF OUR FAITH

The One who initiates and completes our salvation

Hebrews 12:2

RADIANCE OF GOD'S GLORY

Demonstrates God's spotless purity

Hebrews 1:3

EXACT EXPRESSION OF GOD'S NATURE

Jesus is fully God

Hebrews 1:3

FIRSTBORN

Affirms Jesus as the Son of God

Hebrews 1:6

FORERUNNER

The One who goes before us

Hebrews 6:20

GREAT HIGH PRIEST

Humanity's representative before God

Hebrews 4:14

GREAT SHEPHERD OF THE SHEEP

The One who safely leads his flock

Hebrews 13:20

HEIR OF ALL THINGS

The One who has control over all creation

Hebrews 1:2

MEDIATOR

The One who stands between perfect God and sinful man

Hebrews 8:6; 9:15; 12:24

MINISTER OF THE SANCTUARY

The One who leads in the activity of worship and priestly ministry

Hebrews 8:2

ATONEMENT

Paid the price for our sin, making it possible for us to be forgiven

Hebrews 2:17

SON OF GOD

Jesus is God, the second member of the Trinity

Hebrews 4:14

PIONEER OF THEIR SALVATION

The Originator of our salvation

Hebrews 2:10

Cloud of Witnesses

Without receiving their full promises in this world, the witnesses throughout Hebrews 11 declared in their lives and deaths that the life of faith in the promising God is worth it. As the apostle Paul put it, "For I consider that the sufferings of this present time are not worth comparing with the glory that is going to be revealed to us" (Rom 8:18). Encouraged by these witnesses, we look to Jesus Christ, and by faith, his victory over sin and death belongs to us all. So let us run the race of faith with endurance.

Abel	By faith, offered a sacrifice approved by God and was murdered by his brother	Gen 4:1–16
Noah	By faith, aligned himself with God and condemned the world in its sin	Gen 6:5–9:17
Abraham	By faith, lived as a foreigner in tents in the promised land	Gen 12–25
	By faith, offered up Isaac, his promised son, as a sacrifice when God tested him	Gen 22:1–19
Isaac	By faith, lived as a foreigner in tents in the promised land	Gen 21–35
Jacob	By faith, lived as a foreigner in tents in the promised land	Gen 25–50
Joseph	By faith, gave the Israelites instructions concerning his bones, though he died outside the promised land	Gen 50:24–26
Moses	By faith, chose to suffer with God's people rather than enjoy the sin of the Egyptians	Exod 2–4
Rahab	By faith, aligned herself with God's people rather than her own disobedient people	Josh 2; 6:22–25
Gideon	By faith, led his army of 300 men against a superior force of over 130,000 men	Judg 7:1–8:12
Samson	By faith, called on the Lord for strength to kill about 3,000 Philistines in an act of self-sacrifice	Judg 16:26–30
Samuel	By faith, confronted King Saul in his sin and anointed David as king in his place	1 Sam 15:10–16:13
David	By faith, ran from King Saul rather than strike down the Lord's anointed until he became king over Israel	1 Sam 16:1– 2 Sam 5:5
The Prophets	By faith, some endured torture, mocking, scourging, imprisonment, stoning, being sawn in two, execution by the sword, homelessness, destitution, and mistreatment that they might gain a better resurrection	Heb 11:35–38
Jesus	Endured the cross, despising its shame, for the joy that lay before him— sitting down at the right hand of God, saving all those who believe in him	Heb 12:2

KEY VERSE

For this is the kind of high priest we need: holy, innocent, undefiled, separated from sinners, and exalted above the heavens. He doesn't need to offer sacrifices every day, as high priests do—first for their own sins, then for those of the people. He did this once for all time when he offered himself. For the law appoints as high priests men who are weak, but the promise of the oath, which came after the law, appoints a Son, who has been perfected forever. Now the main point of what is being said is this: We have this kind of high priest, who sat down at the right hand of the throne of the Majesty in the heavens, a minister of the sanctuary and the true tabernacle that was set up by the Lord and not man.

○

HEBREWS 7:26–8:2

The Supremacy of the Son: The Chiastic Structure of Hebrews 1:1–4

What is a **chiasm**? It's a literary technique in which an author arranges a sequence of ideas or words that repeat themselves in the second half in reverse order, like in the case of Hebrews 1:1–4, which has an ABCDDCBA pattern. By arranging these truth statements like this, the author was not only observing some parallels about the person, office, and work of the Son of God but also placing special focus on the Son's identity—namely, as one who shares the same glory and nature as God the Father (v. 3). This arrangement fit with the author's larger purpose in Hebrews to demonstrate the unmatched supremacy of Jesus, the Son of God.

A (1:1–2a)—*Long ago God spoke to our ancestors by the prophets at different times and in different ways. In these last days, he has spoken to us by his Son.*

B (2b)—*God has appointed him heir of all things*

C (2c)—*and made the universe through him.*

D (3a)—*The Son is the radiance of God's glory*

D' (3b)—*and the exact expression of his nature,*

C' (3c)—*sustaining all things by his powerful word.*

B' (3d)—*After making purification for sins, he sat down at the right hand of the Majesty on high.*

A' (4)—*So he became superior to the angels, just as the name he inherited is more excellent than theirs.*[9]

James

Genre | **EPISTLE**

The implanted word of truth, which is the
gospel, has opened up to Jesus's followers a
new and wise way of living righteously.

INTRODUCTION

AUTHOR   James is named as the author in 1:1. A number of New Testament personalities were named James, but only three are candidates for the authorship of this book: James the son of Zebedee, James the son of Alphaeus, and James the brother of Jesus (also called James the Just). This James is identified as the brother of Jesus in Matthew 13:55; Mark 6:3; and Galatians 1:19. James later led the Jerusalem church (Gal 2:9,12), exercising great influence there (Acts 1:14; 12:17; 15:13; 21:18; 1 Cor 15:7; Gal 2:9,12).

BACKGROUND   James was probably written between AD 48 and 52, though nothing in the epistle suggests a more precise date. James's death in AD 62 or 66 means the epistle was written before this time. Similarities to gospel traditions and Pauline themes are suggestive. If Mark was written around AD 65 and time is allowed for the events of Acts 15 and 21 to have occurred between Paul's first and second missionary journeys, a date between AD 48 and 52 seems most likely. James led the Jerusalem church. The reference to "the twelve tribes dispersed abroad" (Jas 1:1) suggests the letter was written to Jewish Christians living outside Israel.

MESSAGE AND PURPOSE   As a general epistle, James was addressed to a broad audience (Jewish Christians) rather than a specific audience (e.g., Christians at Ephesus only). There is an obvious concern to address internal and external difficulties being faced by Jewish Christian congregations. James addressed these issues primarily through the application of principles defined by the Old Testament wisdom tradition. The solutions he named reflected the wisdom from above that comes from the "Father of lights" (1:17) who gives wisdom generously to those who ask for it.

SUMMARY   The book of James is a wonderful companion piece to the teachings of Jesus as recorded in the four Gospels. James has a strong ethical emphasis that is consistent with the moral teachings Jesus gave to his disciples. Like Jesus's teachings, the book of James is a source of exhortation and comfort, reproof and encouragement.

STRUCTURE   The book of James is a letter (an epistle), though only the greeting conforms to the ancient Greek form exemplified in Paul's letters, especially Galatians. The book of James has been compared to Old Testament Wisdom literature. While there are wisdom elements in James, such as comparing the wisdom of the world with the wisdom that comes from God, it also contains exhortations and prophetic elements not common to Wisdom literature.

Outline

prautēs

Greek pronunciation:
[prah OO tays]

CSB translation:
gentleness

Uses in James: 2
Uses in the NT: 11

Focus passage:
James 3:13

Prautēs (*gentleness, humility*) always appears as a positive quality in the NT. Christians are encouraged to receive *humbly* the implanted word able to save their lives (Jas 1:21). This inward attitude of *gentleness* always manifests itself outwardly. There is no such thing as a *gentle* attitude that does not express itself in *gentleness* with relation to others. Therefore, good conduct should operate in the *gentleness* that wisdom requires (3:13). *Gentleness* is a fruit of the Spirit (Gal 5:23). Christians are to clothe themselves with *gentleness* not only toward one another (Col 3:12) but also toward all people (Titus 3:2). Sinners are to be restored in a spirit of *gentleness* (Gal 6:1). The servant of God is not to quarrel even with his opponents. Rather, he is to instruct them in *gentleness* with a view to their repentance (2 Tim 2:24–25; cp. 1 Pet 3:16).

huperēphanos

Greek pronunciation:
[hoo pehr AY fah nahs]

CSB translation:
proud

Uses in James: 1
Uses in the NT: 5

Focus passage:
James 4:6

In the NT, *huperēphanos* appears exclusively in an unfavorable sense, referring to one who is *haughty* or *arrogant*, always in relation to other people. Thus, people show their *pride* by foolishly refusing to submit to God and authorities. Consequently, God opposes them (Luke 1:51; Jas 4:6). God is opposed to the *proud* believer who resists those in authority and acts *arrogantly* toward his fellow brothers and sisters (1 Pet 5:5). Thus, *huperēphanos* represents a *pride* of heart that manifests itself through a state of demeaning others. Paul's use of *huperēphanos* supports this conclusion. Twice he lists the term in a vice list (Rom 1:30; 2 Tim 3:2).

JAMES

Analogies in James

Analogy comes from a compound Greek word that means "between sayings or expressions." The word indicates a comparison between two things, a comparison that highlights similar features or attributes, things that might otherwise be considered dissimilar.[10] The challenge for the biblical interpreter is first to understand and identify the literal or physical reference and then to transfer some part of that meaning to the object of comparison. The astute reader must slow down and ponder more carefully the author's message.

UNPRODUCTIVE BECOMES PRODUCTIVE

JAMES 1:10–11 • JAMES 3:12 • JAMES 5:7–8

NATURE

JAMES 3:3 • JAMES 3:5 • JAMES 3:7–8 • JAMES 3:11–12

SOCIOECONOMICS

JAMES 2:6 • JAMES 4:13–14

EVERYDAY LIFE

JAMES 1:15 • JAMES 2:26 • JAMES 5:2

But be doers of the word and not hearers only, deceiving yourselves. Because if anyone is a hearer of the word and not a doer, he is like someone looking at his own face in a mirror. For he looks at himself, goes away, and immediately forgets what kind of person he was. But the one who looks intently into the perfect law of freedom and perseveres in it, and is not a forgetful hearer but a doer who works—this person will be blessed in what he does.

JAMES 1:22-25

1–2 Peter & Jude

Genre | **EPISTLE**

Because of their heavenly identity, inheritance, and hope obtained through Jesus's resurrection, Christians should pursue holy and distinct lifestyles even while enduring persecution and suffering as they seek to imitate Jesus (1 Peter). Christians should seek to grow in the grace and knowledge of Jesus because of the truthfulness of the gospel message, which is rooted in Scripture and confirmed by the apostolic eyewitness, recognizing the threat of false teaching and the temptations of this world (2 Peter). The presence of false teachers who promote licentiousness and deny Jesus's lordship means that true believers must uphold the apostolic faith passed down to them (Jude).

INTRODUCTION

AUTHOR The author of 1 Peter identified himself as "Peter, an apostle of Jesus Christ" (1:1). He viewed himself as a divinely ordained, directly commissioned, authoritative representative of the Lord Jesus himself. Several statements in the letter indicate that the Peter who plays a prominent role in the Gospels is the author (2:21–24; 5:1). The author of 2 Peter plainly identified himself as the apostle Peter (1:1). He called himself "Simeon Peter" (1:1), a name not generally used of the apostle (elsewhere only in Acts 15:14). In 2 Peter, Peter may have borrowed some from Jude, or both may have used a common source. All these evidences suggest that 2 Peter should be accepted as authentic. Jude called himself "a servant of Jesus Christ and a brother of James" (Jude 1). Most likely Jude referred to the well-known leader of the Jerusalem church (Acts 15:13–21; Gal 2:9). This is significant, for this James was the brother of Jesus (Mark 6:3). If Jude was a brother of James, then he was also a brother of Jesus.

BACKGROUND First Peter was probably written sometime between AD 62 and 64. While Paul was under house arrest from AD 60 to 62, he did not refer to Peter in Rome. Peter likewise did not mention Paul as being in Rome; only Silvanus and Mark were his companions (5:12–13). These facts suggest that Peter wrote 1 Peter sometime after AD 62 and before the writing of 2 Peter. Unlike 1 Peter, 2 Peter does not mention specific recipients or refer to an exact destination. The apostle referred to his epistle as the "second letter" he had written to his readers (2 Pet 3:1). Peter likely wrote 2 Peter from Rome, where church tradition placed the apostle in his latter days. Because he mentioned that his death was near (1:14), it seems the letter was written just before his death. The readers of Jude's letter were probably Jewish Christians because of Jude's several references to Hebrew history. Beyond this information we do not know exactly who the recipients of Jude's letter were.

MESSAGE AND PURPOSE Peter wrote to encourage suffering believers in Asia Minor to stand firm for Christ in the midst of persecution. In 1 Peter, he urged them to do so by focusing on their spiritual privileges and, more specifically, the place where their rights and privileges lay: the next life. In 2 Peter, Peter cautioned believers to beware of false teachers with their bogus doctrines and licentious lifestyles. The temptation to a sinful lifestyle so concerned Peter that shortly after his first letter, he followed up with this one. Jude had originally meant to write a letter on salvation to his friends. But he changed his plans when he learned of false teachers who had infiltrated the church (vv. 3–4). Jude reminded his readers that they shared a common salvation and alerted them to the need for vigilance in contending for the faith.

SUMMARY First Peter provided encouragement to suffering believers living in northern Asia Minor who faced intense persecution. The letter encourages faithfulness while under oppression. In 2 Peter, Peter wrote to warn against false teachers and the negative influence they can have on moral living. The letter emphasizes true knowledge of God while facing false teaching and encourages readers to maintain Christian virtue in the midst of the world's vice. Jude sought to protect Christian truth and strongly opposed heretics who threatened the faith. The letter's message is relevant to any age because believers should defend the gospel vigorously. Jude bears an obvious similarity in content with 2 Peter, a book that also deals firmly with false teachers who were infiltrating the church.

STRUCTURE The structure of 1 Peter has been the subject of discussion from the earliest history of the church. The diversity of outlines illustrates that the task of exegesis is not merely a science but also an art. Second Peter is a general letter with the typical features of a salutation, main body, and farewell. What is missing is an expression of thanksgiving. The letter of Jude is a vigorous and pointed piece of writing. The letter bears the marks of a careful and disciplined structure and was directed to specific circumstances in the life of the church.

Outlines

1 PETER

I. **Greeting (1:1–2)**

II. **Called to Salvation as Exiles (1:3–2:10)**
   A. Praise for salvation (1:3–12)
   B. The future inheritance an incentive to holiness (1:13–21)
   C. Living as the new people of God (1:22–2:10)

III. **Living as Strangers in a Hostile World (2:11–4:11)**
   A. The Christian life as a battle and witness (2:11–12)
   B. Testifying to the gospel in the social order (2:13–3:12)
   C. Responding in a godly way to suffering (3:13–4:11)

IV. **Persevering in Suffering (4:12–5:11)**
   A. Suffer joyfully in accord with God's will (4:12–19)
   B. Exhortations to elders and the community (5:1–11)

V. **Concluding Words (5:12–14)**

2 PETER

I. **Greeting (1:1–2)**

II. **Building on Faith with Godly Qualities (1:3–11)**

III. **The Apostle Peter's Testimony (1:12–21)**

IV. **Warning against False Teachers (2:1–22)**

V. **Certainty of Christ's Return (3:1–10)**

VI. **Christ's Return Impels Us to Holy Living (3:11–18)**

JUDE

I. **Greeting and Purpose (vv. 1–4)**

II. **Description of the False Teachers (vv. 5–19)**

III. **Exhortation to Faithfulness (vv. 20–23)**

IV. **Doxology (vv. 24–25)**

hierateuma

Greek pronunciation:
[hee eh RAH tyoo mah]

CSB translation:
priesthood

Uses in 1 Peter: 2
Uses in the NT: 2

Focus passage:
1 Peter 2:5,9

Hierateuma (*priesthood*) first appears in written literature in the Greek OT (Exod 19:6; 23:22). If Israel obeyed God, she would be his treasured possession (Exod 23:22) and would function as a royal *priesthood* through which God would dispense his blessing to the whole earth (Exod 19:5–6; 23:22). In the NT, Peter makes direct reference to Exodus 19:6 and 23:22 and applies the fulfillment of this OT concept of *royal priesthood* to the church (1 Pet 2:9), which now exists to serve God by worshipping him through her words and deeds. She is being built into a spiritual temple where believers perform the role of a holy *priesthood* by offering "spiritual sacrifices acceptable to God through Jesus Christ" (2:5). The church also serves God through the proclamation of the praises that belong to him (2:9).

hupsoō

Greek pronunciation:
[hoo PSAH oh]

CSB translation:
exalt

Uses in 1 Peter: 1
Uses in the NT: 20

Focus passage:
1 Peter 5:6

Hupsoō refers to *lifting* something to a higher location. As Moses *lifted up* the serpent in the wilderness, Christ was *lifted up* on the cross (John 3:14). This concept of *lifting up* is figuratively extended to mean *to exalt* or *honor* (raising something to a position of higher status). In the example above, the *lifting up* of Jesus referred to his crucifixion (cp. John 8:28) but also to his *exaltation* (cp. John 12:32). The one who possesses the higher authority must be the one who *exalts* others to a higher status (Luke 1:52; Acts 2:33; Jas 4:10; 1 Pet 5:6). He made the people of Israel *prosper* in Egypt (Acts 13:17), and he *exalts* the humble (Matt 23:12 = Luke 14:11; Luke 18:14). Elsewhere, Paul humbled himself so that those in the Corinthian church might be *exalted* (2 Cor 11:7).

tartaroō

Greek pronunciation:
[tahr tah RAH oh]

CSB translation:
cast into hell

Uses in 2 Peter: 1
Uses in the NT: 1

Focus passage:
2 Peter 2:4

The verb *tartaroō* means *to throw down into Tartarus*. Its only NT occurrence (2 Pet 2:4) refers to God casting disobedient angels into *Tartarus*, an idea with a Homeric parallel. Well before NT times, Homer (ca. eighth c. BC) spoke of *Tartarus* as a subterranean place of punishment where Zeus banished the Titans (a family of ruling gods; Hom. *Il.* 14.279). Hesiod (ca. 8th c. BC) remarked that "a brazen anvil falling from earth nine nights and days would reach Tartarus upon the tenth" (Hes. *Theog.* 724–5). It is a dark, dank place "under misty gloom," surrounded by a bronze fence—a place "which even the gods abhor" (Hes. *Theog.* 730, 739). Eventually, *tartaroō* made its way into Jewish apocalyptic literature, retaining the idea of a place of punishment. It appears closely equivalent to Jewish *gehenna* (*hell*) (Syb. *Or.* 4:186), which supplies the Jewish background alluded to in 2 Peter 2:4. Thus, *tartaroō* carries the sense of *cast into hell* in this context.

1–2 Peter & Jude Timeline

2085–1406 BC

2085?
Destruction of Sodom and Gomorrah

1446
The exodus

1409?
Balaam's error

1406
Moses's death

250 BC–AD 29

WINTER 5 BC
Jesus's birth

AD 1?
Simon Peter born in Galilee, probably in Bethsaida

5
Birth of Jude, half-brother of Jesus

20?
Simon, a fisherman by trade, moves to Capernaum.

29
Jesus calls Simon Peter "the rock."

29
Jesus calls Peter to be one of his 12 disciples.

AD 30–33

32
Peter's confession at Caesarea Philippi that Jesus is the Messiah

33
Peter, James, and John witness Jesus's transfiguration.

33
Peter vows to die with Jesus.

33
Peter denies Jesus in the courtyard of Annas.

AD 33–47

NISAN 14–16
Jesus's trials, death, resurrection, and ascension (or April 3–5, AD 33)

33
Following his resurrection, Jesus appears to Peter and recommissions him.

33
Three thousand respond to Peter's sermon at the feast of Pentecost.

OCTOBER 34
Saul's conversion on the Damascus road

37?
Paul meets with Peter and James on his first visit to Jerusalem following his conversion.

44
James becomes leader of the church at Jerusalem.

AD 48–65

48–52
The letter of James written

49
At Antioch, Paul confronts Peter's refusal to share meals with Gentile believers.

62
James, the half-brother of Jesus, stoned to death

AD 66–70

66
The letter of Jude written

66
Peter's martyrdom in Rome

66–70
Jewish war

70
Destruction of Jerusalem

AD 96–180

96
Jude's grandsons appear before Emperor Domitian.

112
Pliny's letter to Emperor Trajan about persecuting Christians

180
Muratorian Canon includes Jude as Scripture.

Comparison: 2 Peter 2 and Jude

THEME	2 PETER	JUDE
False teachers and ungodly people will exploit and turn people from God.	There were indeed false prophets among the people, just as there will be false teachers among you. They will bring in destructive heresies, even denying the Master who bought them, and will bring swift destruction on themselves. Many will follow their depraved ways, and the way of truth will be maligned because of them. They will exploit you in their greed with made-up stories. Their condemnation, pronounced long ago, is not idle, and their destruction does not sleep. *2 Peter 2:1–3*	For some people, who were designated for this judgment long ago, have come in by stealth; they are ungodly, turning the grace of our God into sensuality and denying Jesus Christ, our only Master and Lord. *Jude 4*
Sinful angels are chained in darkness.	For if God didn't spare the angels who sinned but cast them into hell and delivered them in chains of utter darkness to be kept for judgment. *2 Peter 2:4*	And the angels who did not keep their own position but abandoned their proper dwelling , he has kept in eternal chains in deep darkness for the judgment on the great day. *Jude 6*
Sodom and Gomorrah serve as an example of what happens to the ungodly.	And if he reduced the cities of Sodom and Gomorrah to ashes and condemned them to extinction, making them an example of what is coming to the ungodly. *2 Peter 2:6*	Likewise, Sodom and Gomorrah and the surrounding towns committed sexual immorality and perversions, and serve as an example by undergoing the punishment of eternal fire. *Jude 7*
God will bring judgment to the ungodly and rescue the holy.	Then the Lord knows how to rescue the godly from trials and to keep the unrighteous under punishment for the day of judgment. *2 Peter 2:9*	"Look! The Lord comes with tens of thousands of his holy ones to execute judgment on all and to convict all the ungodly concerning all the ungodly acts that they have done in an ungodly way, and concerning all the harsh things ungodly sinners have said against him." *Jude 14b–15*
Defiling the flesh	Especially those who follow the polluting desires of the flesh and despise authority. *2 Peter 2:10*	In the same way, these people—relying on their dreams—defile their flesh, reject authority, and slander glorious ones. *Jude 8*
Godly angels are guardians who don't speak evil against sinners.	However, angels, who are greater in might and power, do not bring a slanderous charge against them before the Lord. *2 Peter 2:11*	Yet when Michael the archangel was disputing with the devil in an argument about Moses's body, he did not dare utter a slanderous condemnation against him but said, "The Lord rebuke you!" *Jude 9*
Evil blasphemes and brings destruction.	But these people, like irrational animals—creatures of instinct born to be caught and destroyed—slander what they do not understand, and in their destruction they too will be destroyed. *2 Peter 2:12*	But these people blaspheme anything they do not understand. And what they do understand by instinct—like irrational animals—by these things they are destroyed. *Jude 10*
Evil is deceitful, destitute, and full of absolute darkness—unlike the light and living water of eternal God.	They will be paid back with harm for the harm they have done. They consider it a pleasure to carouse in the broad daylight. They are spots and blemishes, delighting in their deceptions as they feast with you. . . . These people are springs without water, mists driven by a storm. The gloom of darkness has been reserved for them. *2 Peter 2:13,17*	These people are dangerous reefs at your love feasts as they eat with you without reverence. They are shepherds who only look after themselves. They are waterless clouds carried along by winds; trees in late autumn—fruitless, twice dead and uprooted. They are wild waves of the sea, foaming up their shameful deeds; wandering stars for whom the blackness of darkness is reserved forever. *Jude 12–13*
Abandonment	They have gone astray by abandoning the straight path and have followed the path of Balaam, the son of Bosor, who loved the wages of wickedness. *2 Peter 2:15*	Woe to them! For they have gone the way of Cain, have plunged into Balaam's error for profit, and have perished in Korah's rebellion. *Jude 11*
Those who walk according to fleshly desires	For by uttering boastful, empty words, they seduce, with fleshly desires and debauchery, people who have barely escaped from those who live in error. *2 Peter 2:18*	These people are discontented grumblers, living according to their desires; their mouths utter arrogant words, flattering people for their own advantage. *Jude 16*

The Day of the Lord

Conduct yourselves honorably among the Gentiles, so that when they slander you as evildoers, they will observe your good works and will glorify God on the day he visits. 1 Peter 2:12

○

We also have the prophetic word strongly confirmed, and you will do well to pay attention to it, as to a lamp shining in a dark place, until the day dawns and the morning star rises in your hearts. 2 Peter 1:19

○

Then the Lord knows how to rescue the godly from trials and to keep the unrighteous under punishment for the day of judgment, especially those who follow the polluting desires of the flesh and despise authority. 2 Peter 2:9–10

○

By the same word, the present heavens and earth are stored up for fire, being kept for the day of judgment and destruction of the ungodly. Dear friends, don't overlook this one fact: With the Lord one day is like a thousand years, and a thousand years like one day. 2 Peter 3:7–8

○

But the day of the Lord will come like a thief; on that day the heavens will pass away with a loud noise, the elements will burn and be dissolved, and the earth and the works on it will be disclosed. 2 Peter 3:10

○

It is clear what sort of people you should be in holy conduct and godliness as you wait for the day of God and hasten its coming. Because of that day, the heavens will be dissolved with fire and the elements will melt with heat. But based on his promise, we wait for new heavens and a new earth, where righteousness dwells. 2 Peter 3:11b–13

○

But grow in the grace and knowledge of our Lord and Savior Jesus Christ. To him be the glory both now and to the day of eternity. 2 Peter 3:18

○

In this, love is made complete with us so that we may have confidence in the day of judgment, because as he is, so also are we in this world. 1 John 4:17

○

And the angels who did not keep their own position but abandoned their proper dwelling, he has kept in eternal chains in deep darkness for the judgment on the great day. Jude 6

○

Stranger Things in General: 2 Peter and Jude in View of Extrabiblical Writings[11]

SECOND PETER IN A SENTENCE: Christians should seek to grow in the grace and knowledge of Jesus because of the truthfulness of the gospel message, which is rooted in Scripture and confirmed by the apostolic eyewitness, recognizing the threat of false teaching and the temptations of this world.

JUDE IN A SENTENCE: The presence of false teachers who promote licentiousness and deny Jesus's lordship necessitates that true believers struggle to uphold the apostolic faith passed down to them.

1) **1 ENOCH 6–19**
   - Book of Enoch: no specific time, date, or place, possibly late third or early second century BC (probably derived from the Book of Noah; included among Old Testament pseudepigrapha)
     - Partly Aramaic, partly Hebrew
     - Development over centuries: large and diverse scope of religious topics
   - Apocalyptic visions of Enoch: intercession on behalf of Azazel and the Watchers
     - Section 1
     - Chapters 6–19 (e.g., 6–7; 10:4–16; 12; 15; 19)
   - **Sample Passage:** "And it came to pass when the children of men had multiplied that in those days were born unto them beautiful and comely daughters. And the angels, the children of the heaven, saw and lusted after them, and said to one another: 'Come, let us choose us wives from among the children of men and beget us children.'" (1 Enoch 6:1–3)

2) **ASSUMPTION OF MOSES**
   - Composite work with the Testament of Moses (ca. AD 7–29)
   - No extant copies—the Assumption portion only is preserved in a few Greek quotations (e.g., Jude 9, Clement of Alexandria, some later Greek writers)
     - Burial of Moses (Deut 34:1–8)
     - Zechariah 3:2, "The LORD rebuke you, Satan!"
   - Emphases on grace instead of human merit, Israel's election and role in history, the messianic kingdom, and Moses's unique relationship to Jewish religion
   - **Sample Passage:** "And do thou, Joshua (the son of) Nun, keep these words and this book; For from my death [assumption] until His advent there shall be CCL times. And this is the course *of the times* which they shall pursue till they are consummated. And *I shall go* to sleep with my fathers. Wherefore, Joshua thou (son of) Nun, [be strong and] be of good courage; [for] God hath chosen [thee] to be minister in the same covenant." (Assumption of Moses 10:11–15)

1–3 John

Genre | **EPISTLE**

Because Jesus is the true God and eternal life that came in the flesh, believers should avoid destructive beliefs and behaviors that deny who he is.

INTRODUCTION

AUTHOR   Ancient manuscripts are unanimous in naming "John" as the author of 1 John. This was understood to be John the son of Zebedee, the "beloved disciple" who was also the author of the Fourth Gospel. The style and vocabulary of 1, 2, and 3 John are so close to that of John's Gospel that they beg to be understood as arising from the same person.

BACKGROUND   Second-century sources reported that around AD 70, the year the Romans destroyed Jerusalem and the temple, John left Jerusalem, where he was a church leader, and relocated to Ephesus. He continued his pastoral work in that region and lived until nearly AD 100. Ephesus is probably the place where John wrote the three New Testament letters that bear his name.

MESSAGE AND PURPOSE   First John was written to confirm Christians in true apostolic Christianity by helping them avoid the destructive beliefs and behaviors to which some had fallen prey. Second John was apparently written to help readers follow through on their commitment to follow Christ. Third John is a personal letter that revolves around three individuals: (1) Gaius, the recipient of the letter; (2) Diotrephes, the one causing trouble; and (3) Demetrius, who was probably the bearer of the letter.

SUMMARY   John's first letter addresses a setting in which some people in the local church had departed the fellowship (2:19), apparently because their doctrine, ethics, devotion, or some combination of these conflicted with those of the church. John wrote in part to stabilize the situation. He reaffirmed and enlarged on key theological truths, particularly the doctrine of Christ. He extolled love and emphasized the necessity for belief to be matched by action. The second epistle of John advises "the elect lady" (either a reference to a congregation or to a woman who owned a house where the congregation met) to be fervent in Christian love (v. 5) and watchful of deceivers (vv. 7–8). The shortest book in the New Testament, 3 John is a letter with a kind but businesslike tone. "The elder" sought to encourage Gaius, who was perhaps a pastor under his oversight.

STRUCTURE   It is widely agreed that 1 John does not logically, methodically, or rigorously set forth and develop its arguments. For this reason scholars are divided on the best way to structurally outline the letter. It is the least letter-like of the three Johannine Epistles because of its lack of identification of the sender and the recipient. Second John is an excellent example of hortatory or exhortative discourse, which has the intent of moving readers to action. It follows the normal New Testament pattern for a letter with an opening, main body, and closing. Third John also follows the basic epistolary pattern with an introduction (vv. 1–4), a body (vv. 5–12), and a conclusion (vv. 13–14).

Outlines

1 JOHN

I. **The Truth about Christ (1:1–4)**
    A. An affirmation about the person of Christ (1:1)
    B. An affirmation about the author of the letter (1:2–4)

II. **The Believer's Lifestyle (1:5–2:14)**
    A. Fellowship with God (1:5–7)
    B. Confession of sin (1:8–10)
    C. Obeying the commands of Christ (2:1–6)
    D. Maintaining relationships with other believers (2:7–14)

III. **The Believer's Relationship to the World (2:15–27)**
    A. Do not love the world (2:15–17)
    B. Beware of antichrists (2:18–27)

IV. **A Message for God's Children (2:28–4:21)**
    A. They will one day be like Christ (2:28–3:3)
    B. They are not to continue in sin (3:4–6)
    C. They must not be led astray by evil (3:7–10)
    D. They are to love one another (3:11–24)
    E. They are to "test the spirits" (4:1–3)
    F. They are to overcome the world (4:4–6)
    G. They are to reflect God's character (4:7–21)

V. **Final Exhortations (5:1–21)**
    A. Obedient love is proof of faith (5:1–5)
    B. Christ brings us eternal life (5:6–15)
    C. God's children do not continue to sin (5:16–21)

2 JOHN

I. **Greeting and Blessing (vv. 1–3)**

II. **Exhortation to Christian Love (vv. 4–6)**

III. **Warnings about False Teachers (vv. 7–11)**

IV. **Impending Visit and Blessing (vv. 12–13)**

3 JOHN

I. **Greeting to Gaius (vv. 1–2)**

II. **Joy at Seeing Christians Demonstrate the Truth (vv. 3–4)**

III. **Pressing Issues (vv. 5–12)**
    A. Support for traveling ministers (vv. 5–8)
    B. The problem of Diotrephes (vv. 9–10)
    C. Commendation of Demetrius (vv. 11–12)

IV. **Impending Visit and Blessing (vv. 13–15)**

koinōnia

Greek pronunciation:
[koy noh NEE ah]

CSB translation:
fellowship

Uses in 1 John: 4
Uses in the NT: 19

Focus passage:
1 John 1:3,6–7

Koinōnia most often carries the sense of *communion* or *fellowship*, referring to an association involving close mutual relations. This idea of mutual involvement is seen in extrabiblical usage, where *koinōnia* can refer to *marriage* (3 Macc 4:6). Because of a common Spirit, Christians have *fellowship* with God and one another (1 John 1:3,6, 7). This kind of intimate *fellowship* was displayed among the sharing community of the early church (Acts 2:42). *Koinōnia* may also refer to the way in which this *fellowship* is portrayed—namely, through *sharing, generosity,* or *participatory feeling*. Paul speaks of the Corinthian church's generosity in *sharing* a financial gift (2 Cor 9:13). By extension, *koinōnia* may refer to the financial *contribution* itself (Rom 15:26). It may also express *participation* or *common fellowship* in a task or cause. Thus, believers have a common *participation* in the faith (Phlm 6) and *sharing* in Christ's body and blood (1 Cor 10:16).

homologeō

Greek pronunciation:
[hah mah lah GEH oh]

CSB translation:
confess

Uses in 1 John: 5
Uses in the NT: 26

Focus passage:
1 John 4:2–3,15

Homologeō (*to confess*) functions in a number of ways in the NT, and it plays an important part in John's theology (nearly 40 percent of its occurrences appear in John's writings). Most often, *homologeō* means *to assert, confess* or *declare publicly* (Matt 7:23; Matt 10:32 = Luke 12:8; John 9:22; 12:42; Acts 23:8). This outward confession is viewed as a window into the person's actual beliefs (Rom 10:10). In this sense, *homologeō* may refer to a public declaration of agreement with some religious *confession* or set of doctrines (John 1:20; Acts 24:14; Rom 10:9,10; 1 Tim 6:12; Titus 1:16). The *confession* spoken of in 1 John 1:9 appears to be private but does not exclude public *confession*. Elsewhere, *homologeō* stresses the idea of an *agreement* or *acknowledgment* about something (Heb 11:13), and it may mean *to assure* or *promise* (Matt 14:7; Acts 7:17) and also *to praise* (Heb 13:15).

eidōlon

Greek pronunciation:
[AY doh lahn]

CSB translation:
idol

Uses in 1 John: 1
Uses in the NT: 11

Focus passage:
1 John 5:21

In the Greek OT, *eidōlon* (*idol*) refers to the physical representation of a god (Exod 20:4; Deut 5:8). By extension, it points not only to that physical representation but to the supposed existing god behind that form. The worship of these *idols* was evidence of that fact (Exod 20:5; Num 25:2; Deut 5:9), and some were even understood to have demonic powers (Deut 32:17). This usage provides the background for the NT use of *eidōlon*. Paul regards *idols* as false gods, powerless compared to the true God (1 Thess 1:9). He acknowledges the existence of demonic powers behind *idols* but understands them to have no real power over the Christian, who knows that *idols* are but false gods (1 Cor 8:4–7; 10:19–21). Christians are exhorted to abstain from association with *idols* and the false gods they represent (Acts 15:20; 1 John 5:21), for there is only one God (1 Cor 8:4).

1–3 John Timeline

AD 17–61

17
Ephesus experiences a destructive earthquake.

52
Paul travels through Ephesus toward the end of his second missionary journey.

52
Apollos comes to Ephesus and is mentored by Aquila and Priscilla.

54
Paul returns to Ephesus for a two-and-a-half-year ministry.

61
Paul writes his letter to the Ephesians.

AD 62–67

62
Timothy, elder of Ephesus, receives first letter from Paul, 1 Timothy.

62
James, the half-brother of Jesus, stoned to death.

64–67?
Peter's and Paul's deaths in Rome

66
The Jewish War is started by Zealots, who drive the Romans out of Jerusalem temporarily.

66–70?
John leaves Jerusalem for Ephesus.

AD 67–70s

67?
Timothy receives second letter from Paul, 2 Timothy.

70
The Romans crush the Jewish rebellion and destroy Jerusalem and the temple.

70–100
John is spiritual leader of the church at Ephesus.

70s
John's Gospel written

AD 80s–100

80s
John's letter (1 John) to the churches of Asia Minor

80s
John's letter to the elect lady (2 John)

80s
John's letter to Gaius (3 John)

95
John is exiled to Patmos and writes the book of Revelation.

100
Ephesus becomes one of the world's largest cities with a population approaching 500,000.

The one who has the Son has life. The one who does not have the Son of God does not have life. I have written these things to you who believe in the name of the Son of God so that you may know that you have eternal life.

○

1 JOHN 5:12–13

Revelation

Genre | APOCALYPTIC (PROPHECY),
EPISTLE (CHAPS. 1–3)

Through a sequence of visions given to John, Jesus addressed
the spiritual state of seven churches in Asia Minor and also
presented with cosmic imagery historical and future events that
the people of God would experience leading up to the new heaven
and new earth that will coincide with Jesus's ultimate return.

INTRODUCTION

AUTHOR The traditional view holds that the author of Revelation is the apostle John, who wrote the Fourth Gospel and the three letters of John. The writer referred to himself as "John" (Rev 1:4,9; 22:8), and he had personal relationships with the seven churches of Asia Minor (1:4,11; 2–3). Further, the author's circumstances at the time of writing (1:9) matched those of John the apostle (who was placed in Asia Minor from about AD 70 to 100 by reliable historical sources from the second century AD).

BACKGROUND The initial audience that received the book of Revelation was a group of seven local churches in southwest Asia Minor (1:11; 2–3). Some of these congregations were experiencing persecution (2:9–10,13), probably under the Roman emperor Domitian (ruled AD 81–96). Others had doctrinal and practical problems (2:6,13–15,20–23). Also behind these surface problems was the backdrop of unseen but powerful spiritual warfare (2:10,14,24; 3:9). Though some scholars have dated the book later and a few have dated it earlier, commonly held dates of Revelation among evangelical scholars are the mid-90s and the late 60s of the first century AD. The mid-90s view is the stronger view, and it is held by the majority of scholars.

MESSAGE AND PURPOSE Much of the book of Revelation focuses on events at the end of the age (eschatology), more so than any other book in the Bible. But it also focuses on practical choices that believers and unbelievers must make in the course of their lives that have far-reaching consequences at the end.

SUMMARY The resurrected, glorified Jesus Christ revealed himself to the apostle John, who had been imprisoned "on the island called Patmos" (1:9). Christ's twofold purpose was (1) to unveil spiritual diagnoses for seven of the churches in Asia Minor with which John was familiar (chaps. 2–3) and (2) to reveal to John a series of visions setting forth events and factors related to the end times (chaps. 4–22).

STRUCTURE The book of Revelation previews its sequential structure in 1:19: "Therefore write what you have seen, what is, and what will take place after this." From the apostle John's vantage point in being commanded to "write," he had already seen the vision of the exalted Son of Man (chap. 1). Next, he was told to "write" letters to the seven churches, telling each the state of its spiritual health (chaps. 2–3). Lastly comes the body of the book (4:1–22:5), which covers all the events that would "take place after this" (4:1).

Outline

I. **Introduction: "What You Have Seen" (1:1–20)**
   A. Prologue (1:1–3)
   B. Salutation and doxology (1:4–8)
   C. The Son of Man and the churches (1:9–20)

II. **Letters to the Churches of Asia: "What Is" (2:1–3:22)**
   A. The church in Ephesus (2:1–7)
   B. The church in Smyrna (2:8–11)
   C. The church in Pergamum (2:12–17)
   D. The church in Thyatira (2:18–29)
   E. The church in Sardis (3:1–6)
   F. The church in Philadelphia (3:7–13)
   G. The church in Laodicea (3:14–22)

III. **Visions of the End Times: "What Will Take Place after This" (4:1–22:5)**
   A. The heavenly throne room (4:1–5:14)
   B. The opening of the seven seals (6:1–8:1)
   C. The sounding of the seven trumpets (8:2–11:19)
   D. The signs before God's final wrath (12:1–14:20)
   E. The seven bowls of God's wrath (15:1–19:5)
   F. The reign of the King of kings (19:6–20:15)
   G. The new Jerusalem (21:1–22:5)

IV. **Conclusion (22:6–21)**
   A. The command not to seal the scroll (22:6–13)
   B. Washing robes and the water of life (22:14–17)
   C. Warning about adding to the prophecy (22:18–19)
   D. Closing assurance and benediction (22:20–21)

pantokratōr

Greek pronunciation:
[pahn tah KRAH tohr]

CSB translation:
almighty

Uses in Revelation: 9
Uses in the NT: 10

Focus passage:
Revelation 1:8

Pantokratōr means *almighty, omnipotent, all-powerful*. In the Greek OT, the word frequently translates the Hebrew *Yahweh tseva'ot* (LORD of Armies), which stresses God's power over forces opposed to him and his people. *Pantokratōr* also translates Hebrew *Shaddai* (*the Almighty*), a term emphasizing God's power and authority over all things. In every instance in the OT, the one true God is in view.

In the NT, every occurrence of *pantokratōr* refers to God the Father. In the book of Revelation, it occurs with the expressions *Lord God* (1:8; 4:8; 11:17; 15:3; 16:7; 19:6; 21:22), *God* (16:14; 19:15), and variations of the phrase "the one who is, who was, and who is to come" (1:8; 4:8; 11:17). John uses these designations (along with many others) to describe the supremacy of God over all things, including human history. God *Almighty* is actively working to bring everything into conformity with his will.

hagios

Greek pronunciation:
[HAH gee ahss]

CSB translation:
holy

Uses in Revelation: 25
Uses in the NT: 233

Focus passage:
Revelation 4:8

Hagios (*holy*) frequently refers to that which is *dedicated* or *set apart* to God's service, describing things that have a derived holiness. This includes the church (1 Cor 3:17; Eph 5:27; 1 Pet 2:9) and individual Christians (Rom 12:1). Indeed, *hagios* may be translated "saints" in reference to believers, who are *set apart* by God for his service (Matt 27:52; Acts 9:13; Rom 1:7; 1 Cor 1:2; Rev 5:8). The word also describes Jerusalem (Matt 4:5; Rev 21:2,10; 22:19), the various parts of the sanctuary (Matt 24:15; Heb 9:1–3), angels (Mark 8:38), OT prophets (Luke 1:70), Christian apostles and prophets (Eph 3:5), divine revelation (Rom 1:2; 2 Pet 1:21), and various geographical locations (Acts 7:33; 2 Pet 1:18). Additionally, *hagios* may describe what is *holy* by nature—namely, God the Father (John 17:11; 1 Pet 1:15; Rev 4:8), Jesus Christ (Mark 1:24; Acts 3:14), and the Spirit (Matt 3:11; Acts 1:5).

thērion

Greek pronunciation:
[thay REE ahn]

CSB translation:
beast

Uses in Revelation: 39
Uses in the NT: 46

Focus passage:
Revelation 11:7

Thērion (*beast, animal*) was used to refer to any living creature, excluding man, but usually wild, *undomesticated animals*. In mythological imagery, *thērion* could describe supernatural creatures such as the griffin, the hydra, or a huge dragon.

In the NT, *thērion* normally refers to *undomesticated animals* in general (Mark 1:13; Acts 11:6; Titus 1:12; Heb 12:20; Jas 3:7), including a snake (Acts 28:4–5) and particularly dangerous animals (Rev 6:8). However, Daniel 7 and most of the occurrences of *thērion* in Revelation (6:8; 18:2 excepted) reflect the more metaphorical, mythological imagery. *Thērion* occurs 10 times in the Greek OT of Daniel 7, where four *creatures* arise from the sea, understood as four Gentile empires (v. 17). Similarly, Revelation uses *thērion* as (1) a vivid personification of an ungodly Gentile empire (17:3), (2) the antichrist (11:7; 13:1–4,17; 17:7–8; 19:19), and (3) the false prophet (13:11).

Book of Revelation

MILLENNIAL PERSPECTIVES

	AMILLENNIAL	POSTMILLENNIAL
General	Viewpoint that the present age of Christ's rule in the church is the millennium; holds to one resurrection and judgment marking the end of history as we know it and the beginning of life eternal	Viewpoint that Christ's kingdom brings about an extended period of human flourishing before Christ's second coming (the 1,000 years not being a precise length of time); holds to one resurrection and judgment marking the end of history as we know it and the beginning of life eternal
Book of Revelation	Church history written in code to confound enemies and encourage Asian Christians; message applies to all Christians throughout the ages	Primarily a history of the past events leading up to the fall of Rome in the fourth century, making the book more of a prophetic outlook on the early centuries of the church; message applies to all Christians throughout the ages
Historical division of Revelation prophecies	All prophecies apply to Roman province of Asia and to all churches of all ages. Chapters 19–22 deal with Christ's bodily, visible return; resurrection; judgment; and the new age.	The majority of the book is a prophetic and symbolic description of events that took place at the time of Jerusalem's fall (chaps. 4–11) and through the time of the Roman Empire's fall in the fourth century (chaps. 12–19); many proponents contend the book was written before AD 70; chapter 20 describes the transition to a golden age of human flourishing because of the gospel's worldwide influence before Christ's return and final judgment (chaps. 21–22).
Rapture	When this word is used by this view, it refers to the second coming of Christ when everyone is resurrected (chap. 20).	When this word is used by this view, it refers to the second coming of Christ, which comes after the 1,000-year reign, when everyone is resurrected (chap. 20).
Conversion of Israel	Refers to new Israel, spiritual Israel, the church	Refers to new Israel, spiritual Israel, the church
Antichrist (chaps. 13; 17–18)	Symbolic forces that oppose God throughout history; sea beast, earth beast, heads, horns, and kings all symbolize aspects of Roman Empire of John's day and also apply to all ages of history	Symbolic forces that oppose God within Revelation primarily refer to figures and movements of the Roman Empire; sea beast, earth beast, heads, horns, and kings all symbolize aspects of Roman Empire of John's day, the beast being a figure that existed in the first century and the antichrist being more of an ongoing heretical movement than a future individual person

	HISTORICAL PREMILLENNIAL	DISPENSATIONAL PREMILLENNIAL
General	Viewpoint that Christ will reign on earth for 1,000 years following his second coming; saints will be resurrected at the beginning of the millennium, nonbelievers at the end, followed by judgment	Viewpoint that after the battle of Armageddon, Christ will rule through the Jews for a literal 1,000 years accompanied by two resurrections and at least three judgments
Book of Revelation	Church history written in code to confound enemies and encourage Asian Christians; message applies to all Christians throughout the ages	Church history written in code to confound enemies and encourage Asian Christians; message applies to all Christians throughout the ages
Historical division of Revelation prophecies	Chapters 1–3 deal with Roman-period Asia and also apply to all churches of all ages; chapters 4–18 deal with events from the crucifixion to the return of Christ and into eternity.	Chapter 1 is current with John. Earlier generations of dispensationalists say chapters 2–3 define historical periods within the church age and also apply to all churches of all ages; the rapture occurs at the end of the church age. Most dispensationalists today say these churches are "historical and representative"—that is, they actually existed in John's time and churches like each of these exist today. Chapters 4–22 deal with events after the rapture of the church.
Rapture	When this word is used by this view, it refers to the second coming of Christ at the beginning of the millennium (chap. 19).	This word is used to refer to the church being caught up out of the earth at the end of the church age (end of chap. 3 and before chap. 4).
Conversion of Israel	Refers to conversion of Jews in the end time, but by grace through faith; nothing changes in gospel presentation (chap. 11)	Refers to conversion of Jews in the end time when the Israelite temple system and Israelite kingdom are reestablished; church age is a parenthesis of history, necessary because Jews rejected Christ (chaps. 11–20)
Antichrist (chaps. 13; 17–18)	Literal person who will appear at the end time, same as sea beast, while heads, horns, and kings indicate his power and his agents; who he is will be apparent at the proper time	Same as earth beast of 13:11, a Jewish leader who will head up apostate religion, working in league with new Rome (a federation of nations that will come out of the old Roman Empire), symbolized in various ways by sea beast, heads, horns, mountains, and kings; who he is will be apparent at the proper time (some dispensationalists equate the antichrist with the sea beast)

Comparison of the Cherubim

CATEGORY	EZEKIEL'S CHERUBIM (BOOK OF EZEKIEL)	JOHN'S LIVING BEINGS (BOOK OF REVELATION)
Basic Description	"four living creatures" (Ezek 1:5)	"four living creatures" (Rev 4:6)
Wings	four (1:6; 10:21)	six (4:8)
Faces**	lion, ox*, man, eagle (1:10; 10:14)	lion, ox, man, eagle (4:7)
Eyes	multiple (1:18; 10:12)	multiple (4:6–8)
Torso	like a man (1:5)	
Feet	like a calf (1:7)	
Hands	like a man (1:8; 10:8,21)	
Movement	rapid, like a flash of lightning (1:14)	
Sound	like the rushing of many waters (1:24)	
Transportation	wheels within wheels for each (1:15–21; 10:9–13)	
	*But in Ezekiel 10, the face of a cherub rather than an ox	**In Revelation, each of the cherubim seems to have one face, while in Ezekiel, each has four faces.

Churches of the Revelation

CHURCH	STRENGTHS	WEAKNESSES	CHALLENGE	TO THE ONE WHO CONQUERS
Ephesus 2:1–7	Right theology, defense of the faith, and moral behavior	Abandoned the love they had at first	Remember how far they had fallen, repent, and do the works they did at first	Jesus will give the right to eat from the tree of life, which is in the paradise of God
Smyrna 2:8–11	Rich in faith despite affliction and poverty	–	Don't fear suffering but remain faithful, even to the point of death	Jesus will give the crown of life, never harmed by the second death
Pergamum 2:12–17	Holding on to Jesus's name without denying their faith in him despite persecution	Some hold to false teachings, living lives of immorality	Repent	Jesus will give some of the hidden manna; he will also give a white stone with a new name
Thyatira 2:18–29	Love faithfulness, service, endurance; last works greater than the first	Tolerating a false prophetess and teacher who encouraged immorality	Those who commit adultery with her must repent; those who don't hold this teaching must hold on to what they have until he comes	Jesus will give authority over the nations, just as Jesus received from his Father; he will also give the morning star
Sardis 3:1–6	A few people have not defiled their clothes (v. 4)	Had a reputation for being alive, but they were dead	Be alert and strengthen what remains, which is about to die; remember what they have received and heard: keep it and repent	Will be dressed in white clothes and name will never be erased from the book of life; will be acknowledged by Jesus before his Father and the angels
Philadelphia 3:7–13	Kept Jesus's word and did not deny his name; kept his command to endure	–	Hold on to what they have so that no one takes their crown	Jesus will make them pillars in the temple of God, never to go out again; Jesus will write on them the name of the city of God and his new name
Laodicea 3:14–22	–	Neither cold nor hot (useful) but lukewarm; self-focused and deceived	Focus on Jesus; be zealous and repent	Jesus will give the right to sit with him on his throne, just as he conquered and sat down with his Father on the throne

The Second Coming

THE FIRST AND SECOND COMINGS OF JESUS CHRIST	
HIS FIRST COMING	**HIS SECOND COMING**
He rode a donkey	He will ride a white horse
He came as the Suffering Servant	He will come as King and Lord
He came in humility and meekness	He will come in majesty and power
He came to suffer the wrath of God for sinners	He will come to establish the kingdom of God for his saints
He was rejected by many as the Messiah	He will be recognized by all as Lord
He came to seek and save the lost	He will come to judge and rule as King
He came as God incognito	He will come as God in all his splendor

All Things New

GOD'S PEOPLE	IN	GOD'S PLACE	UNDER	GOD'S RULE
Adam and Eve		Eden		God's Command

ADAM AND EVE SINNED—EXILED FROM THE GARDEN

GOD'S PEOPLE	GOD'S PLACE	GOD'S RULE
Abraham	Canaan	Abrahamic Covenant
Israel under Moses	Promised Land	Mosaic Covenant
Israel under Monarchy	Promised Land	Mosaic Covenant, Davidic Rule

ISRAEL SINNED—EXILED FROM THE PROMISED LAND

GOD'S PEOPLE	GOD'S PLACE	GOD'S RULE
Prophetic Faithful Remnant	Prophesied Restored Land	Prophesied New Covenant

JESUS CHRIST OBEYED—INAUGURATED THE NEW COVENANT

GOD'S PEOPLE	GOD'S PLACE	GOD'S RULE
Christians, Those "in Christ"	New Heaven and New Earth, New Jerusalem Where Christ Dwells	New Covenant, Christ's Rule

Sources

[1] This information and its arrangement is drawn primarily from Michael J. Kruger, *Canon Revisited: Establishing the Origins and Authority of the New Testament Books* (Wheaton, IL: Crossway, 2012), 266–80.

[2] Andreas J. Köstenberger and Scott R. Swain, *Father, Son and Spirit: The Trinity and John's Gospel* (Downers Grove, IL: InterVarsity Press, 2008), 187.

[3] "Paul," *Holman Illustrated Bible Dictionary, Revised and Expanded* (Nashville: B&H Publishing, 2015), 1228.

[4] Ibid.

[5] Ibid.

[6] N. T. Wright and Michael F. Bird, *The New Testament in Its World* (Grand Rapids, MI: Zondervan Academic, 2019), 467.

[7] D. Edmond Hiebert, *The Thessalonian Epistles: A Call to Readiness* (Chicago: Moody Press, 1971), 307.

[8] Knute Larson, *I and II Thessalonians, I and II Timothy, Titus, Philemon* in *Holman New Testament Commentary* (Nashville: Holman Reference, 2000), 106.

[9] This specific chiasm is taken from Lane G. Tipton, "Christology in Colossians 1:15–20 and Hebrews 1:1–4: An Exercise in Biblico-Systematic Theology," in *Resurrection and Eschatology: Theology in the Service of the Church: Essays in Honor of Richard B. Gaffin Jr.*, ed. Lane G. Tipton and Jeffrey C. Waddington (Phillipsburg, NJ: P&R, 2008), 179–80, with CSB text inserted.

[10] "Analogy" in Richard N. Soulen and R. Kendall Soulen, *Handbook of Biblical Criticism*, 4th ed. (Louisville: Westminster John Knox Press, 2011), 7. Adapted from Steve Booth, "Analogies in the Book of James," *Biblical Illustrator*, Fall 2013, 63–67. © Lifeway Christian Resources. Used by permission.

[11] John D. Barry, ed., *Faithlife Study Bible* (Bellingham, WA: Lexham Press, 2016); Robert Henry Charles, ed., *Pseudepigrapha of the Old Testament*, vol. 2 (Oxford: Clarendon Press, 1913); George W. E. Nickelsburg, *1 Enoch: A Commentary on the Book of 1 Enoch, Chapters 1–36; 81–108*, ed. Klaus Baltzer (Minneapolis: Augsburg Fortress, 2001).